PREPARING TO STUDY ABROAD

PREPARING TO STUDY ABROAD

Learning to Cross Cultures

Steven T. Duke

Forewords by Steven S. Reinemund and Ken Bouyer

STERLING, VIRGINIA

Figure 1.1, "The Cultural Iceberg," is provided courtesy
of Language & Culture Worldwide (www.languageandculture.com).
Copyright © 2010 by Language & Culture Worldwide, LLC

Published by Stylus Publishing, LLC.
22883 Quicksilver Drive
Sterling, Virginia 20166-2102

Library of Congress Cataloging-in-Publication Data

Duke, Steven Taylor, 1965-
Preparing to study abroad : learning to cross cultures / Steven T. Duke.
pages cm
Includes bibliographical references and index.
ISBN 978-1-57922-993-1 (cloth : alk. paper)
ISBN 978-1-57922-994-8 (pbk : alk. paper)
ISBN 978-1-57922-995-5 (library networkable e-edition)
ISBN 978-1-57922-996-2 (consumer e-edition)
1. Foreign study. 2. Intercultural communication. I. Title.
LB2375.D85 2014
370.116'2—dc23

                                                            2013024657

13-digit ISBN: 978-1-57922-993-1 (cloth)
13-digit ISBN: 978-1-57922-994-8 (paperback)
13-digit ISBN: 978-1-57922-995-5 (library networkable e-edition)
13-digit ISBN: 978-1-57922-996-2 (consumer e-edition)

Printed in the United States of America

All first editions printed on acid-free paper
that meets the American National Standards Institute
Z39-48 Standard.

Bulk Purchases

Quantity discounts are available for use in workshops and for
staff development.
Call 1-800-232-0223

First Edition, 2014

10   9   8   7   6   5   4   3   2

Dedicated to the hundreds of thousands of students who study abroad each year.

CONTENTS

ACKNOWLEDGMENTS

I wish to acknowledge the hundreds of students at Wake Forest University who have studied abroad and participated in one of the three cross-cultural engagement courses we offer. I have had the privilege of teaching many of them. It is with deep gratitude that I thank those students who agreed to let me publish some of their reflections and observations in this book.

In addition, I gratefully recognize the research and contributions of many scholars who have studied and written about culture. In particular, I appreciate the kind words of encouragement from Michael Vande Berg, who is one of the pioneers in using research and results to shape and reshape how intercultural learning is taught in study abroad.

I also wish to express my appreciation to John von Knorring and the dedicated staff at Stylus Publishing. It has been a pleasure to work with them as this book comes to fruition. I also appreciate the assistance of Jim Lance in catching the vision of the manuscript and helping me transform it into something that I hope will be useful to others.

Finally, I express my deep gratitude to Kristin, Alan, Jonathan, and Evie for their patience and support throughout the writing and revising of this book and to my parents, James and Ruth, for their support for, insights into, and encouragement of my own overseas experiences. Of course, I bear full responsibility for all of the errors and omissions contained in this book.

FOREWORD I

Steven S. Reinemund

Today we live in a global marketplace. Are we appropriately preparing our college graduates to enter this workplace?

Very few students who are educated in the United States today enter college with a global perspective or even an appreciation for the cultural differences that exist in the United States, much less around the world. Along with the classroom rigors of higher education there is a real need to provide our young people with a genuine understanding of and appreciation for cultural differences. This should include the mastery of another language.

It is not until we truly internalize the differences in our cultures that we can understand how to be good citizens of the world. Many of us grew up in monolithic communities where the Golden Rule was, "Treat others as you would like to be treated." This makes a lot of sense when others live similar lives with common purposes, values, and needs. A friend of mine recently shared the notion that we need to operate with the Platinum Rule: "Treat others as they would like to be treated." In a diverse and inclusive world, this Platinum Rule makes more sense. To be able to practice it we must truly understand and respect the cultures of others.

In my role as the CEO of multinational company, the importance of incorporating a rigorous international experience in the academic curriculum of our college students became quite clear to me because so many in the workplace lacked that foundation. An experience in another culture will not prepare a student to master every cultural challenge; but, if done correctly, an international experience will provide a student with an appreciation for the value of what people with completely different world-views can bring to life situations.

I highly recommend that college students include a well-planned and rigorous international immersion experience in their college curriculum. This book makes an excellent starting place for embarking on this vital transformative journey.

Steven S. Reinemund
Dean, Wake Forest University School of Business
Retired Chairman/CEO, PepsiCo

FOREWORD 2

Ken Bouyer

It's a matter of perspective: Recognizing yours, then expanding it. What you get out of your studies, career, and even life itself is largely grounded in the way you perceive the world. And no matter your perspective, you don't have to look far to see that globalization is everywhere. The ability to function in a global economy is vital, and it hinges on your perspective. What's needed in this dynamic world is inclusive leaders who have a global mind-set.

You will work in a truly global world. Chances are that the companies where you'll begin your careers will be multinational. These organizations have a global perspective and recognize that difference matters. In return, they expect their people to think globally and lead inclusively, allowing everyone to bring their full selves to work. Without grasping and delivering on these expectations, we can't offer exceptional client service, a key differentiator in the global marketplace.

But maybe you're reading this thinking that you don't need to concern yourself with such clients, because you're an entrepreneur. Well, first off, thanks; this world needs you. But second, and more importantly, a global mind-set and inclusive leadership still play an important part in driving innovation. Your supply chain may have links in Beijing and Brussels. Or you may draw your funding from someone born outside the United States. As globalization continues, the chances increase immensely.

To develop these skill sets, it's important that you, as a student in today's world, ask yourself, "Am I prepared to go beyond borders? To leave my comfort zone?"

You're reading this book, so I can only assume you are. Good for you—the business world needs talented individuals, those who take the initiative to expand their mind-set and leadership style and see the world through a broader lens. The alternative? Let globalization wash over you and then wonder what happened. Those who choose the former will emerge as business leaders. They'll be the ones affecting global markets.

So how do you identify them, these globally minded, inclusive leaders? I'd bet that you could look in a mirror. We emphasize three aspects, or kinds of *capital*, as defined by the Thunderbird School of Global Management's Najafi Global Mindset Institute (n.d.): intellectual, psychological, and social. Like it sounds, *intellectual capital* refers to knowledge: cognitive complexity, global business savvy, and a cosmopolitan outlook. Are you self-assured and adventure-seeking, with a passion for diversity? If so, you've got a lot of *psychological capital*. People with significant *social capital* are diplomatic, demonstrate intercultural empathy, and have strong interpersonal relationships.

Those who can see business broadly—not just from a singular perspective—*those* are the graduates that companies seek and the kind of professionals that advance. Like globalization, learning is continuous. By studying abroad, you've got a jump on that. Keep that momentum—it should continue throughout your career and life.

The great thing about a global mind-set and inclusive leadership, however, is that you can develop these skills without crossing any borders. That brings me to my final point: Start right there, at college. The university setting offers you a safe environment in which you can expand your mind-set.

To stretch beyond your perspective, look within your classrooms. Who's there? Where are they from? What are their experiences? Have candid conversations with people different from yourself and see how you're alike—and how you're not. Both are important. Like my seventh-grade social studies teacher had on her wall: "Different does not necessarily mean deficient."

University is a great place to learn beyond the classroom, too. Join a campus organization that takes you outside of your comfort zone. If you aren't Asian, join an Asian group, or another organization that will expand your experiences. College organizations can be rich in culture and wellsprings of global knowledge. Chances are, students from these groups are eager to learn about your culture, too!

Even seemingly benign things can broaden your perspective. Listen to foreign newscasts on TV or online. Watch a foreign film. Read an international newspaper. Grab some friends and try a new ethnic restaurant. As small as these activities seem, they go to show how simple it is to develop your global mind-set and act inclusively.

I'm sharing these things because I want to impress upon you the importance—maybe even the *urgency*—of asking yourself, "How do I get beyond the walls of my university?"

If you're studying abroad, that's one way. But taking even that a step further, go beyond the book-learning; immerse yourself in the culture, customs, and norms of another place. Being overseas is a tremendous opportunity. And translating that experience and perspective into today's business world, it's a tremendous advantage. Clients want business partners who think globally and act inclusively. Your time to prepare is now.

Good luck, and all the best in your endeavors!

Ken Bouyer

Director of Inclusiveness Recruiting, Ernst & Young, LLP

Reference

Thunderbird School of Global Management, Najafi Global Mindset Institute. (n.d.). Global mindset inventory's three capitals. Retrieved from http://globalmindset.thunderbird.edu/home/global-mindset-inventory/three-capitals

PREFACE

In today's uncertain economy, study abroad is a valuable experience for any college student. Kudos to you for even considering study abroad as an option. Students who study abroad develop valuable knowledge, skills, and insights about the world that will serve them well in today's globalized economy, in the world of business, non-profits, graduate school, and interactions in the community. Many employers are seeking employees who have the intercultural skills, knowledge, and awareness of other parts of the world that can come from traveling and studying abroad.

So what is the value of study abroad? And how can the process of traveling to a foreign country help you develop intercultural skills, knowledge, and awareness? In my opinion, there are numerous positive influences. Here is a short list of reasons why you should consider traveling abroad to study, perform an internship, or conduct an in-depth research project. Doing so can help you do the following:

- Learn about other countries firsthand, including their political, historical, economic, social, and religious features
- Study a foreign language and develop your language abilities
- Develop your communication skills and ability to interact with people who speak other languages
- Develop respect, patience, and cultural sensitivity for people from other cultures
- Learn new approaches to your academic discipline
- Understand yourself and your own cultural values, habits, and expectations with greater clarity
- See up front how people live in other parts of the world

- Learn about international transportation and communication systems and how to navigate in new or unfamiliar environments
- Learn how to observe and act in situations where actions, behaviors, and the unwritten rules of communication are unclear
- Develop resilience and resourcefulness
- Gain experience in dealing with ambiguity

Thousands of students have returned from studying abroad and reported having "amazing" or "transformational" experiences. They often describe how being abroad opened new awareness in them of other countries and peoples, and they want to see more of the world. This group includes those who have been privileged to travel abroad with family before college, as well as those who never had a passport before deciding to study abroad.

Although it is hard to pinpoint everything these students mean when they say they have been transformed, it is likely a combination of personal development plus newfound insights regarding the sights, food, music, and artistic products of other cultures, in addition to a newfound maturity and confidence in their own ability to navigate the world at large. In addition, it is likely that studying abroad has stimulated new development in them. A recent study found that the process of studying abroad might lead to rewiring in the brain and the development of new synapses and memories (Fischer, 2013).

Many employers recognize the value of study abroad and the skills, knowledge, and insights it can develop in those who have traveled abroad. A recent study by IES Abroad, one of the oldest and largest study abroad program organizers, found that returned study abroad students reported that they earned starting salaries approximately $7,000 above the national average of $28,000 for starting salaries of recent college graduates. In addition, 89% of the returned study abroad students in the study reported getting their first job within six months of graduation (Preston, 2012). Other studies have also found positive correlations between study abroad and its influence on the development of interpersonal skills and career advancement (Dwyer, 2004; Norris & Gillespie, 2009). A recent survey of 367 companies in nine different countries found that the vast majority ranked intercultural skills highly among potential new employees. The intercultural skills most highly valued by the organizations studied were demonstrating respect for others, working effectively in diverse teams, understanding cultural differences, and adjusting communication to fit different situations (British Council, Ipsos Public Affairs, & Booz Allen Hamilton, 2013).

The concepts contained in this book are intended to help you prepare carefully and intentionally for your study abroad experience and to develop intercultural skills and awareness. The focus in this volume is on culture and the process of learning about and exploring cultural differences and similarities. Unfortunately, many students go abroad without taking the time to learn about their host country and culture, and they often miss valuable opportunities to meet local people and learn firsthand about important elements of the local cultures. Being intentional about your preparation will make you better prepared for the numerous opportunities that study abroad affords. Chapter 1 describes general aspects of crossing cultures and cross-cultural engagement. Chapter 2 provides a list of strategies for making cross-cultural interaction work for you. Chapters 3 and 4 are devoted to some of the outwardly visible aspects of culture, whereas Chapters 5 and 6 explore less visible aspects of culture that require observing the locals up close. Chapter 7 covers issues of identity, and Chapter 8 offers insights about the cultural adjustment process and "culture shock."

In Chapter 9, as well as other chapters, you will find reflections of students who describe a few of their many experiences abroad. Reflecting about your interactions with your hosts is an important aspect of intercultural learning and awareness. Whether you do this in writing, in conversation with your hosts, or in conversation with fellow students you meet in your program, it is only through reflection—upon your interactions and the motivations and actions of yourself and others—that you actually make meaning out of those interactions. The goal is to make the study abroad experience as meaningful, rewarding, and insightful as possible. Safe travels!

INTRODUCTION

Congratulations on your decision to study abroad. This year approximately 270,000 U.S. college students and thousands of high school students will study abroad, and thousands more will travel abroad to participate in research, an internship, a service project, an athletic competition, a musical or artistic performance, or some other activity. This book is written for you, the students who are learning about the world firsthand, who are taking time to see the people and places you have learned about, to conduct the research and perform the service that you have planned for months or years. As you do so, you are changing the world in small but significant ways.

As you travel the world and see sights from Barcelona to Berlin to Beijing, you will have numerous opportunities to interact with the locals. You will be an ambassador, for the United States and/or your home country, for your college or university, for your family, and for your ethnic or cultural group. Study abroad advisors, directors, and faculty across the country trust that you will represent us well and be a good ambassador. We hope you will take advantage of the opportunities to meet people, form friendships, and change perceptions of people both here and abroad. Your family probably has similar goals for you.

One of the most challenging aspects of studying abroad today is meeting the locals and interacting with them in personal, meaningful ways. Many people expect that dropping in on a new city and country will be easy, that getting around will be seamless, and that locals will naturally welcome them with open arms. The reality is that meeting people and getting past "hello" is more difficult than we might expect, especially if we stay for just a few weeks or months. All of us need to adapt our thinking and behavior as we enter a new country or travel to an environment that is different

1

from what we are familiar with. If we don't change our behavior, we often miss out on opportunities to interact with the locals and form friendships. We might misunderstand the local perspective or offend people. As a result, the entire abroad experience can feel incomplete or less satisfying than we had expected.

Many students deal with the stress of living in a new environment by staying in a "bubble," surrounding themselves with the food, people, language, and technology from home. They hang out with other students from home, speak English or their native tongue outside of class rather than the local language, and talk regularly with friends and family back home. Although cell phones, the Internet, Skype, and other technologies make it easy for students to speak with family and friends on a daily basis, they also make it possible for them to remain inside a bubble, unengaged with the people they came to meet.

Study abroad advisors and directors want you to use your experience abroad to see the world through different eyes, learn about different ways of life, and engage with local people and their concerns. Although we realize you want to travel and see many parts of the world, we also hope you will invest time in meeting the people, interacting with them on a personal level, and understanding how they see the world. In doing so, you will find both similarities and differences between the ways they approach life and the way you see the world. If you invest the time, you will have opportunities to form friendships and change attitudes. Many study abroad students have reported that the time spent with their newfound friends was the greatest highlight of their time abroad.

This book is intended to help you deal with and learn from **three main challenges** that are common to the study abroad experience. These are posed as questions to encourage you to think of answers that work for you.

First, how can you interact effectively with people in your study abroad country (the host culture) in personal and authentic ways?

Second, what can you do to step outside the bubble and meet the locals, learn about their interests and attitudes, and see life from their perspective? Can you adjust your strategies based on what works for you?

Third, what can you do to avoid making stereotypes about people in your host culture and instead form generalizations concerning both similarities and differences?

Each person may find his or her own unique ways to respond to these challenges and answer these questions. What works for a student studying in London for four weeks may not work for a student who is performing an internship in Singapore or Cape Town for a semester. A student from a small town or suburb in the United States may need to make more adjustments to life in a big city in Europe than would someone else who grew up in a large city and is traveling to a city of similar size in Asia or Latin America.

In other words, this book is intended to help you with your own personal journey. Education abroad is a wonderful time to learn about yourself, to form new friendships, and to learn of people and places that are both wonderful and challenging. Interacting with the people in your host culture can make all the difference between a fun time and a truly remarkable and life-changing experience abroad. This is your journey. Make the most of it!

WHAT IS CROSS-CULTURAL ENGAGEMENT?

Profile 1: Pamela

As I sit in the library swamped with work, I find myself wishing I were back in London where the library closed at midnight and "flat gathers" were a regular nightly occurrence. I can still remember my first day in London when my nerves were high and I had no idea what to expect. As I sit here now, I realize how much I have grown over these past few months and the huge differences that I see in myself. For one, I am way more independent than I ever was before. I still can't believe that I planned entire trips, from getting to the airport to getting back to my host university, all by myself. Taking planes from place to place made me grow up and experience the responsibility of an adult. This experience was one of the only times where I had to make decisions for myself and did not have others' influences. I honestly could do whatever I wanted and truly got to make decisions based on the things that I desired. The independence and confidence that I gained abroad speaks volumes, as I am able to do many things that I have never done before.

After coming back from abroad, I have learned the importance of culture. I always thought that culture was important, but actually living in another culture showed me the differences between two distinct cultures. It showed me that cultures value different aspects and allowed me to be more open. I am a science major, therefore to me, in many situations, there is just one clear-cut answer. But going abroad allowed me to open up and to see a different perspective. I lived with 10 other students from different places in Europe and the United States and who all had different views of the purpose, meaning, and importance of life. There was not one view that was wrong or better than the rest but rather different. For example, my best friend from abroad is a lacrosse player from a different college. Everything that she does is truly focused around sports, and lacrosse

5

takes precedence over everything. I am completely different. Many things keep me going. I have learned that I value my academic career, strive to be a successful doctor, and, most important, realize that family and friends are the best thing in an individual's life.

While abroad, I saw the connection of extended family and working as a unit through a weekend in the Cotswold visiting my British friend. She made it apparent that everyone chips in on the farm and works as a team. As I learned about this, I realized that I am built in a very similar way. Since I do have a large family, there truly is no "I" in my family. We all work together in order to be successful and will do anything to help each other out. Thus, I have realized that I am never alone in my decision making or any events because I have the support of my friends and family.

Going to London has taught me a lot about my own desires and wishes. After this past year, I have really found my passion and have gained the determination to do well. This is one of the first times in my life that I actually know what I want to be when I grow up, and I feel like I am on the right track. London helped me find this, as I was able to learn about myself through interaction with others. All of us who lived in the same flat would share stories from our own culture, and it really forced me to look at my own culture and see the things that I valued. Our entire "group" full of both Americans and Europeans had individual qualities that defined who we were. I was always classified as the nice, quiet, intelligent American from the group. This allowed me to realize that I do fit into this mold, but it is not the only thing that I value in life. It made me realize that I wanted to show more of myself than just the academic side and that I was composed of other important qualities. Overall, I have learned a lot about myself and the things that have defined me as a person. London helped me develop as a person and become more mature.

As you prepare to study abroad or travel overseas for work, research, service, or teaching, it is a great time to explore the concept of cross-cultural engagement. It is also a great time to learn about yourself and the cultural values, habits, expectations, and assumptions that shape you. At Wake Forest University, we have been teaching a course to help students prepare for their experience abroad. We adopted the term *cross-cultural engagement* to describe the interactions of students who live in another country or culture. The following is our working definition:

> Cross-cultural engagement is a process of learning to interact with individuals in another culture. Engagement implies an active, two-way process of communicating with individuals in

the host culture, rather than simply learning about them from a distance. It also suggests active learning while crossing into another culture.

One of the things we emphasize in the course is the critical need to meet people, interact with them, and begin to see the world from their perspective. We often show a photo or two of visits to homes in different countries, emphasizing that our goal for our students is for them to meet the locals, eat a meal with them, and get to know them. Many returning students have related that some of their best memories from abroad are of the time spent with the locals, forming friendships and learning of their perspectives on life. Pamela, the student who wrote Profile 1, found that the time spent with students in her flat (or apartment) was one of the best parts of her experience in London. Other students return from abroad and tell us that they regret that they did not engage much with the people in their study abroad location but spent their time with students from their home school. Interacting with your hosts is essential and will enable you to see the things you share in common with them, as well as the differences in how you act and experience the world around you.

Preparing yourself to travel to another country is important for so many reasons. It can help you learn about food, music, art, traditions, and other aspects of culture that may be different from your own. It can help you understand the history, political and social systems, and economy of your host country. And it can prepare you to meet and understand a variety of people along the way and to interact with them frequently. I hope you will read this book with an open mind, asking yourself the questions posed throughout the book in order to explore your own expectations and values. Reflecting on your own habits and expectations is a critical part of your preparation, because doing so can help you identify what you expect of yourself and of others. It can help you prepare emotionally, psychologically, and spiritually for an experience that opens your mind to new possibilities and ways of thinking.

Preparing for your study abroad experience will also help you emotionally for the inevitable differences between how you live your life and how life functions in other parts of the world. What many call "culture shock" (see Chapter 8) can also be labeled as "transition shock," because it happens when moving from a familiar system of expectations, habits, and values into a system where the expectations and values may be different or unclear. It is part of the process of adjustment to a different location and mode of life. The chapters that follow cover a wide range of topics intended to help you prepare for this transition. Although many people will tell you that culture shock can be a good thing, it is nevertheless a shock because the stresses of life in a different culture challenge the expectations you have of yourself and others.

What is the value of studying or working abroad? There are so many reasons to study abroad in the twenty-first century. Today's world is becoming increasingly globalized, and many corporations and industries are becoming integrated across continents. Although it was common just two generations ago for most production and consumption to take place locally, now it is common for companies to buy products made halfway around the world for use here and for U.S. companies to build items for export. The U.S. workforce is also becoming more international, making it essential for employees to possess and use a variety of intercultural skills. Students who study or travel abroad learn firsthand how the economies, political systems, and social networks function in other parts of the world. In addition, study abroad students have the opportunity to view different cultures up front. Cross-cultural understanding can be a powerful force that strengthens relationships despite our differences. In contrast, cross-cultural misunderstandings have led to tension, anger, lost contracts, numerous missed opportunities, and even war. Studying abroad can help you develop transferable intercultural skills that you can use later in your career and personal life.

It may be helpful at this stage to define *culture*. Many scholars have written about culture from a variety of perspectives. You may have already taken a course on cross-cultural communication, psychology, or anthropology where you studied a variety of definitions. Anthropologists, historians, sociologists, psychologists, communication specialists, and "interculturalists" have devoted countless pages to the study of humans and their communities. Here are four different authors' descriptions of the term:

Culture refers to values, beliefs, attitudes, preferences, customs, learning styles, communication styles, history/historical interpretations, achievements/accomplishments, technology, the arts, literature, etc.—the sum total of what a particular group of people has created together, share and transmit. (Paige, 2002, p. 43)

[In] spite of many differences in detail, anthropologists do agree on three characteristics of culture: it is not innate, but learned; the various facets of culture are interrelated—you touch a culture in one place and everything else is affected; it is shared and in effect defines the boundaries of different groups. Culture is man's medium; there is not one aspect of human life that is not touched and altered by culture. This means personality, how people express themselves (including shows of emotion), the way they think, how they move, how problems are solved, how their cities are planned and laid out, how transportation systems function and are organized, as well as how economic and government systems are put together and function. (Hall, 1976/1981, pp. 16–17)

[Culture is] an integrated system of learned behavior patterns that are characteristic of the members of any given society. Culture refers to the total way of life of particular groups of people. It includes everything that a group of people thinks, says, does and makes—its systems of attitudes and feelings. Culture is learned and transmitted from generation to generation. (Kohls, 2001, p. 25)

Culture is the relatively stable set of inner values and beliefs generally held by groups of people in countries or regions and the noticeable impact those values and beliefs have on the peoples' outward behaviors and environment. (Peterson, 2004, p. 17)

Viewing these descriptions together allows us to see certain common elements that are useful for study abroad students. First, they make it clear that culture includes things that are visible to the naked eye (technology, the arts, literature, etc.), as well as elements that are less visible (values, beliefs, attitudes, customs, expressions of emotion, etc.). For students going abroad to study or do research, this implies the need to observe the behaviors and attitudes of local people in day-to-day interaction, in addition to learning about the foods, music, arts, technology, and other outward manifestations of their cultures.

Second, these descriptions explain that a culture is shared by a group of people and is transmitted from one generation to the next. Although cultural traditions and values do change over time, they generally change slowly. In most countries there are multiple cultures that coexist at the same time, each one being shared and modified by individuals in the area. We often talk about national cultures, such as "Chinese culture" or "French culture," thinking that everyone within a country shares the identical cultural values and attitudes. However, this way of thinking can get us into trouble when observing culturally driven behaviors, because we may assume that everyone's actions are motivated by the same beliefs and attitudes. If we stop to think about this, we will realize that not everyone in the United States shares the same values and beliefs. So why should we assume that people in other countries share identical attitudes? Instead, we should assume that multiple cultures thrive in most countries.

Scholars have used different metaphors to explain how the outwardly visible and less visible aspects of culture tend to operate and influence behavior. The metaphor that is most widely used to describe culture is the iceberg (Paige, Cohen, Kappler, Chi, & Lassegard, 2002; Peterson, 2004; Storti, 2009). As we know, a portion of an iceberg is visible above the waterline, yet something like 90% of an iceberg is submerged. In this metaphor, the portion of the iceberg that is above the waterline represents the visible aspects of a culture, such as food, clothing, music, transportation, and architecture. But there are many other aspects of how people live, act, and believe that are below the proverbial "waterline." Chapters 5 and 6 delve into a few of the many behaviors, habits, expectations, and values that one could describe as less visible aspects of culture and behavior. Figure 1.1, which was developed by Language & Culture Worldwide, LLC, and is used here with grateful permission, describes the visible aspects of culture as "observable." Observable aspects of culture include behaviors and practices that are apparent to the casual observer. Figure 1.1 describes the less-visible aspects of culture as "not observable," including the interpretations members

Figure 1.1 The Cultural Iceberg.

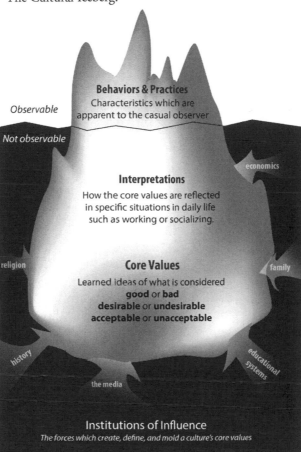

Note: Copyright 2010 by Language & Culture Worldwide, LLC, www.languageandculture .com/cultural-iceberg. Reproduced with permission.

of a culture have for any aspect of daily life, as well as the core values that shape those interpretations. It also reminds us of the numerous influences that shape these core values and interpretations, including religion, history, the media, educational systems, family, and economics.

Other metaphors have also been used to describe culture, including an onion, which has multiple layers that must be peeled off to uncover what is inside; and a tree, which has visible leaves and branches that depend on a healthy root system that is generally unseen by the naked eye.

How can you identify these "underwater" or less visible elements of another culture? Interaction and observation are required to notice and understand them. One of your main goals when going abroad is to begin to explore those "hidden" elements of cultural values, beliefs, and interpretations. The main method for doing so is to meet and interact with the people who live where you will be staying. Can you really expect to understand values and beliefs without meeting the locals, discussing their society, and learning about their traditions and experiences? Will you be able to understand the actions of others without asking them to describe why they do certain things? Of course not. Cross-cultural engagement requires you to interact with your hosts and share your life with them. This two-way communication should be fun and enriching for both parties.

I like the term *cross-cultural engagement* for many reasons. It expresses a sense of direction. Crossing into another culture implies movement, both physically and intellectually. Engagement implies active interaction and opening the mind and the heart to truly understand others. In addition, it encourages interaction on a practical, day-to-day kind of level, beyond just knowing about cultural differences, especially the differences that are most readily apparent, such as food and clothing.

Other terms have also been used to describe one's ability to interact effectively with individuals from other cultures. It is useful to consider some other perspectives as you prepare to study abroad. Hammer, Bennett, and Wiseman (2003, p. 422) used the term *intercultural competence* to describe "the ability to think and act in interculturally appropriate ways." *Intercultural proficiency* is the term preferred by the Association of College Unions International to describe "the ability to successfully communicate, understand and interact among persons with differing assumptions that exist because of ethnic and cultural orientations" (ACUI, 2012).

All of these imply the three areas of knowledge, skills, and attitudes, or head, hands, and heart. Janet Bennett (2008) described these as the "mindset" (cognitive competencies), "skillset" (behavioral competencies), and "heartset" (affective competencies). Darla Deardorff (2006) identified the combined influence of essential attitudes, knowledge and comprehension, and skills in the development of intercultural competence.

As you prepare to study or travel abroad, I encourage you to consider ways that you can increase your understanding of the people who live where you will study. How can you prepare yourself to understand and appreciate their values, interpretations, beliefs, and habits? What goals will you set for spending time with individuals in your host culture? It is much easier to gain a better understanding of people in your host culture and to develop long-lasting intercultural skills when you interact with them and not rely on the observations of others. The following chapters will guide you in considering aspects of cross-cultural learning that you may not have considered previously. Reflecting on your experiences with people from other cultures will help you develop cross-cultural awareness, as well as appreciation for the values and accomplishments of people in other cultures.

2

WHY CROSS-CULTURAL ENGAGEMENT IS OFTEN LIMITED, AND SOME STRATEGIES TO INCREASE IT

Profile 2: Cana Noel

My study abroad experience has had a major impact on my life. I have gained so many skills that I know will help me in my future career and in life in general. I have become a more patient person, I have improved my communication skills, and I am more aware of the norms of other cultures. Without this study abroad experience, I would not know how cultures in other parts of the world operate. Ghana was such a great place to go because of the strong connection people have to their ethnic groups. There are multiple groups in Ghana, and each tribe has a different language and culture and different values and belief systems. I got the opportunity to spend time with people from all of the different ethnic groups. I learned so much about myself in Ghana from my various experiences.

The biggest change I can see in myself is being able to adapt quickly to a new environment. I am the kind of person who always likes to stay in my comfort zone, and I am hesitant to just jump into new things. In Ghana I had no choice but to adapt and embrace everything around me because Ghana became my home for over a month. I learned to love the food, the music, the people, and everything else in my surroundings. Initially I resisted having to adapt to a new place by always comparing everything I saw to home. I did this daily, and one day I realized that I would be wasting my time there if I continued to search for things that reminded me of home. I eventually learned to appreciate everything and understood that although things were not akin to home, they were unique and special in their own way.

I believe that my goals and values have definitely changed since I've been in Ghana. I have learned to take the time out to appreciate what I have, especially my environment and my family. Here in the United States, academics has always been the most important thing because I want to get a good, stable job. However, while living in Ghana I learned to love life and the people in it. I now try to spend more time with my family and friends and just take a moment to be thankful for everything I have. I also value the basic necessities I have access to, such as clean water, food, sanitation systems, and, most important, health care. Many people in Ghana lacked these basic things, and I never realized how much I took some of these things for granted. I came to this realization the first day I realized I could not brush my teeth with the water there or the days when the electricity went off. I am truly grateful for living in a country that provides these basic services.

My five-year plan consists of finishing my undergraduate degree and going to law school. After law school I am not sure what type of law I will pursue, but I hope that it will give me the chance to travel again. I would love to go back to Ghana and live there for a year. I also plan to stay in touch with the people I met, and I enjoy meeting new people from Ghana and discussing my experience. Overall, this trip was one of the best experiences of my life, and I am so thankful to my parents for giving me the opportunity to go.

In the introduction, we discussed three main challenges that are common to the study abroad experience. First, how can you interact effectively with people in your study abroad country? Second, what can you do to get outside "the bubble"? And third, what can you do to avoid stereotyping people in your host country and instead form generalizations based on your own observations? Meeting and interacting with your hosts is essential for students interested in making the most of their study abroad experience. Cana (Profile 2) got out of the bubble by interacting with many people in Ghana. This chapter explores several strategies that can be used to help you get out of "the bubble" while you are abroad.

Why is cross-cultural engagement often limited among study abroad students? I have identified four main reasons. First, many students assume that people in other countries live by the same values and patterns they do, even though they are aware of visible cultural differences. They may see that others eat different food, create and play different music, and wear different types of clothing. And they may be aware that other countries and cultures have had a different history than our own. But until they begin interacting with people from another country or culture on a personal level, they have a hard time identifying what is similar and what is different in how people there think and act.

This assumption that others live by the same values and expectations you do is the first reason why cross-cultural engagement is often limited among study abroad students. You might see people going about their daily activities in another country and assume that you know the motivations and values behind their actions. However, until you confirm or change those assumptions by interacting with your hosts, the assumptions can be misguided or even completely wrong.

A second reason why cross-cultural engagement is often limited is that study abroad students generally have a limited knowledge and understanding of their host country's history, society, geography, religion, politics, and languages. This leaves them less informed about the reasons why cultural values may differ from their own, as well as the values and expectations that may be similar. Although many study abroad programs are available to students with elementary or intermediate language skills, it is also true that improved language ability can make a wider range of conversations possible.

A third reason is that students often ignore opportunities to learn experientially while they are abroad. Although the main mode of learning in the first years of life and school is through direct personal experience, by the time students arrive in college, they often focus primarily on "book learning" and less on observing the people around them. Experiential learning implies that people pay attention to details and adjust assumptions and actions based on what they observe and learn in various situations. This is a critical skill for study abroad students to use actively. Incorrect assumptions and limited knowledge of other countries can leave students unable to notice details that contradict their assumptions.

Perhaps the main reason why cross-cultural engagement is limited among study abroad students is that they have had few opportunities to interact with people from the host country prior to departure. This leaves them uncertain about the expectations and assumptions that are common among the people they will interact with when abroad. It reinforces the assumptions they may have made regarding their hosts. It often perpetuates stereotypes that highlight negative aspects of cultural difference and ignores positive aspects and similarities. Unfortunately, many U.S. American students spend very little time with local people even while in the host country, making it hard for them to get to know their culture in any depth.

Of course, there are numerous solutions for these challenges, solutions that increase cross-cultural engagement and interaction and can reduce misunderstanding. These solutions hinge on the notion that students need to spend more time interacting with local people, more time observing their culture and values face-to-face, more time speaking their language, and more time learning about their history, society, arts, and traditions.

Boiling this down further, we provide a quick list of strategies that we will discuss more in this chapter. This list is not exhaustive. You will likely identify additional strategies of your own.

1. Learn more about your host country and its culture before you leave home.
2. While abroad, find personal, authentic ways to meet local people and interact with them.
3. Learn about culture and cultural values and expectations.
4. Learn about yourself (develop self-awareness) and your own cultural values and expectations.
5. Become a "culture sleuth." Watch for times when people act according to a different set of values or expectations than you use or when "the rules" are different.
6. Show respect when people or situations are different from what you expect.
7. Reflect on what you have observed.

8. Improve your language abilities. Don't rely solely on English or your native language to interact with the locals.
9. Learn how to learn experientially.
10. Have fun!

Strategy 1: Learn More About Your Host Country and Its Culture Before You Leave Home

There are numerous ways you can learn more about your host country. One of the easiest ways is to begin reading a local newspaper or watching a news program on a regular basis. Finding (and using) a dependable source of news and information about the city or region where you will study is an important way to become better informed about the economic, political, educational, and artistic issues of concern there. Of course, many U.S. students today read a newspaper or watch a news broadcast sporadically, even at home. But many foreign newspapers and television news programs are now online, and an increasing number of programs are available through cable or satellite providers.

In addition, take a course (or two or three) about your host country before you go. Faculty in a wide range of disciplines know a lot about the history, language, literature, politics, economy, social groups, science, architecture, arts, music, and urban planning of the country where you will study. Take advantage of courses that expose you to the world and give you in-depth knowledge about the people where you plan to study. You'll feel more confident about their history, society, and culture when you arrive.

If you can't find a course that you can take, or didn't take time for one in previous years, then read at least one or two books about the history and current status of your host country. Travel guidebooks generally contain very limited information about your host country's past and the present-day social, economic, political, and artistic trends. So rely on a travel guidebook for touristy things, such as hotels, restaurants, museums, and other places to visit. But find and read at least one history of the country, plus other books about political, social, religious, economic, artistic, or other issues today. In particular, learn about the things that interest you so you can talk confidently with others about those issues. See the appendix for suggestions of information you may want to learn before you go abroad.

Strategy 2: While Abroad, Find Personal, Authentic Ways to Meet Local People and Interact With Them

In my experience, one of the main goals students have for studying abroad is to meet and get to know the people in another part of the world. Unfortunately, many U.S. students studying abroad spend a significant amount of time traveling on their own, and this means they spend less time in the city where they are studying. If you want to know the people, you need to take the time to meet and get to know them. This implies that you make it a priority to spend time with people, rather than simply travel across the country or region to see the sights.

One great way to meet local people is to participate in a language exchange, where you meet with a local person for two or three hours per week, speaking his or her language for part of the time and English for the rest of the time. If your study abroad program arranges this kind of language and cultural exchange, take full advantage of it. Many students resist language exchanges, if they think their language abilities are weak. Avoid that tendency, and enjoy the chance to practice your language, make some linguistic mistakes, and begin seeing the world through this other person's eyes. Take advantage of the opportunities to ask your language exchange partners about their country and heritage, how they spend their time, what they value, and how their culture functions. Seize any opportunity to go with them to an event or to get a snack, where you can learn new vocabulary and insights related to daily activities such as ordering food. You will notice expectations and attitudes that are similar to your own and a few that are different.

Another common way to meet locals shows up in your housing arrangements. Many U.S. students study abroad at a foreign university, where they have the option to live in a dormitory or residence hall with students of the same university. I always encourage students to live with a foreign student if possible rather than with another U.S. student, because doing so gives you a front-row seat to observe how others live their lives. Some study abroad students live in local apartments, often with students from the same program, but have a local individual assigned as a resident assistant (RA). If you have an RA, take advantage of opportunities to interact with that person weekly, if not daily. Mealtime is a great time to talk and learn about each other. You will also help dispel common misconceptions others have of U.S. American students.

One of the best ways to meet locals is to live in a home stay. If your program offers a home stay, take it! Seriously, get over your fears and hesitations and take advantage of this tremendous opportunity to see the world from a different perspective. Naturally, students who live in a home stay only get as much out of the experience as they invest in it. Some families consist of a single woman living alone, whereas other families are led by just one parent. Some families have children who live in the home, whereas others have children who are grown and have left the home. When I lived in Russia, I had the chance to live with two Russian families for about four months total. I gained insights and learned perspectives about their lives that I would have missed if I had lived on my own. I still remember one of my host "moms" finding Russian movies on television, watching them with me, then sharing her insights into the characters, plot, and culture revealed in these films. Along the way, I learned more about her experiences in life and what she valued. The memories of those conversations are still fresh in my mind, even years later.

Another way to interact with locals is to find a conversation partner or speak with people throughout the day. Of course, this does not need to be formally arranged like a language exchange. Just take advantage of opportunities for conversation with those around you, whether at a local restaurant or café, in a cafeteria or dining facility at the host university, or with a shopkeeper in your area. Many cities have outdoor markets, where local people sell their produce and other goods in an open arena. Taking one or two minutes to ask shopkeepers about their produce or goods not only reinforces language learning but also provides additional information about the local economy and sources of food and products. It will get you off the beaten path and let you see things the tourists miss. Eating at the same cafeteria or café may also provide you with opportunities to speak with those who work or eat there.

Strategy 3: Learn About Culture and Cultural Values and Expectations

Cross-cultural engagement implies that you learn about culture in the broader sense and that you begin looking for the values and expectations that are hidden within each culture, including your own. Numerous books have been written about culture and the many ways to study it. Students who have taken an anthropology or sociology course have been exposed to several ways to approach this subject. Many study abroad programs encourage students to use the "What's Up With Culture" website or to find a book or resource on the host country or culture. Thousands of students have benefited from *Maximizing Study Abroad*, a volume developed by University of Minnesota researchers to help students develop language skills and cross-cultural awareness while studying abroad (Paige, Cohen, Kappler, Chi, & Lassegard, 2002).

In addition, this book has been designed to provide a broad overview of culture and to describe a few situations where cultural values become noticeable. Read this book, explore the strategies described here, and then share what you learned with a friend.

Strategy 4: Learn About Yourself and Your Own Cultural Values and Expectations

Another key to cross-cultural engagement is self-awareness. You have been shaped by many values and expectations during the course of your life. These values have, in turn, shaped your identity and assumptions. In fact, we all have multiple identities and belong to many different groups. For example, one student might be an athlete, a member of a Christian church, active in a sorority or fraternity, and pursuing a specific major. In addition, that student's family upbringing and structure will affect his or her identity, such as being an only child, an oldest child, or perhaps one of many children. Another student might be active in a social group or student government, pursuing a different major, and interested in a less commonly taught language. Some students actively participate in their Jewish, Muslim, Buddhist, Christian, or other faith tradition, whereas others spend little time thinking about religion. In other words, each of us belongs to multiple groups or subgroups, each of which imparts a variety of social and cultural expectations.

Students in the STEM disciplines (science, technology, engineering, mathematics) might have different identities revolving around their interests in biology or chemistry or things they build, models they develop, or scientific habits they acquire. Many of us form identities based on racial, religious, political, or social groups to which we belong, and most of us take identities from social groups to which our parents belong.

As you think about the groups to which you belong, try to identify the kinds of hidden expectations and values you share with each group. For example, are there specific activities or behaviors that the group participates in or expects of its members? Students who are active in sports, music, or theater generally attend practice or rehearsal on a regular basis, and the coach or leader generally expects that the group act in certain ways or avoid other behaviors. This gives some hints regarding how behaviors and values are established and communicated, as individuals form an identity around that activity.

The key to unpacking your own identity (or identities) and the values that go with it is to observe your own behavior in action. What motivates you to do the things you do on a daily or periodic basis? Do certain behaviors bring you joy or fulfillment? If so, why? Are you motivated by goals that lie in the future? If your goals for your future self are fuzzy or unclear, how do you spend your time and with whom? We value hundreds of things, and our behaviors usually put greater emphasis and time on those values. Common values include love for family, love for self, love for one's heritage within a group, independence, group cohesion, love for God or deity, respect for life, respect for others and their property, being self-sufficient, spending time with friends, spending time with family, or being part of a group with a purpose. The list goes on and on.

The critical part of cross-cultural engagement is to avoid the assumption that everyone abroad shares your same identities and values. It is healthy to assume that others have numerous identities and values that motivate them and that their values lead them to act in different ways than you do. Chapter 7 explores identities in greater detail.

Strategy 5: Become a "Culture Sleuth"

Studying abroad offers daily opportunities to see values and behaviors in action. The key is to become more conscious of how local people act differently than you do and then to seek to understand the values that shape those expectations and behaviors. Think of this as becoming a detective or sleuth who has the task of noticing the little things that may be different from what is expected and searching for the reasons behind those differences. Sometimes the differences in behavior will be stark and quickly noticed, whereas other times it will take numerous interactions before you notice something that is different.

A good place to start with your culture sleuthing is to observe the many ways people greet each other and what they say and do when they leave each other. In some places, both men and women who know each other will greet each other with a kiss on the cheek. Pay attention to the patterns for how this is done. Do they kiss on the right cheek first or the left cheek? How many kisses are given when meeting each other, and is this ritual repeated identically when they leave each other? Do the rules for this change if people are of different ages or genders? Are you expected to behave in the same way, or will your status as an outsider mean you are not expected to follow the same patterns? Keep in mind that in some cultures, physical contact is frowned upon, particularly between men and women.

Although it is fun to find patterns and then guess about the rules for such behaviors, it is also appropriate to ask others why they do things and what rules they follow. When you notice something that seems different from what you had expected, find someone to ask. In many cases your study abroad program director or student life staff will enjoy talking with you and helping you with your culture sleuthing. A conversation partner, home stay family member, or fellow student may also have insights for you. Oddly enough, the more you observe and learn, the more you will notice, both about similarities and about differences. Finding "cultural informants" who can help you understand what you have observed will fuel your learning, and you'll have fun in the process.

Strategy 6: Show Respect When People or Situations Are Different From What You Expect

This is probably something your parents or schoolteachers taught you at an early age. It is also an important intercultural skill to learn and practice. Showing respect implies that you avoid attacking or criticizing people when they act differently than you expect. It suggests that you ask questions and seek to understand another person's behavior, rather than get angry or defensive. Showing respect also implies being patient and observant while a new situation unfolds. I am talking not about situations that are dangerous or where your personal safety or health is at risk but about situations that feel different from what you expect. If you feel that you are in danger, it is best to get out of the situation immediately.

One common area where U.S. students often feel awkward or uncomfortable relates to your personal space and how close you stand to another person when having a conversation. In the United States, we often stand 18 to 20 inches apart and have a fairly large "personal zone" around us. When someone comes too close to us in a normal conversation, we tend to move backward in order to preserve our personal space. In some countries it is common for people to stand 12 inches apart or even closer. Showing respect in such situations does not imply that you suddenly change your deeply held attitudes about how much personal space you need. Rather, it suggests that you understand that this behavior is acceptable, even expected, in another culture.

Another example stems from what people wear on their feet at home. In many countries people remove their shoes or boots at the door and immediately put on a pair of slippers or house shoes. The reasons for this vary from place to place, but often it relates to the goal of keeping the home clean. In Russia, streets are sometimes dirty, and this pattern of removing shoes at the door is intended to keep the dirt at the door. Showing respect for local customs means doing your best to observe local practices and follow them as much as you can. This doesn't mean it won't feel awkward (or cold) to remove your shoes immediately when entering an apartment or home, but it does mean making an effort. Other examples regarding differences in common behavior relate to whether people eat meals as a group using their fingers, how they interact with their environment, and dozens of other daily or routine activities.

Showing respect is a key part of several important intercultural skills, such as adaptability, tolerance for stress, flexibility, and dealing with ambiguity. If you regularly make an effort to interact with local people, you will encounter situations where you need to adapt your behavior or thinking. You will naturally feel stress about a variety of things, including speaking the language and dealing with situations where people act differently than you would expect or where the rules of communication are ambiguous. See Chapters 4 and 5 for some examples of this.

Strategy 7: Reflect on What You Have Observed

When you notice something that is different from what you had expected, it is helpful to reflect on those observations. Students who develop the habit of keeping a journal or writing a blog on a regular basis find that doing so helps them focus more on the details of how local people talk and behave. Keeping a journal and reflecting on your experiences can also help you explore your own reactions to different interactions or events. For example, if someone assumed you would act in one way and you assumed you would act in another, how did the exchange make you feel? Did your actions or responses seem to fit the situation? Or do you think you should have done something different?

Some people who keep a journal choose to focus primarily on what they did, whereas others spend more time writing about how they felt or what they thought. Any approach you take is fine. Some prefer to keep a private journal or diary where they can describe deeply personal feelings or emotions, whereas others tend to write for family or friends, particularly if they are writing a blog. Of course, there are various options for you to use, from using paper-based journals and notebooks to saving files on a laptop or a cloud-based network. Some students prefer to integrate photos with text, such as in a blog, whereas others keep them separate.

Keep in mind that reflecting on experiences can also be done in a group setting. Some study abroad programs plan weekly or regular opportunities for group discussion and reflection. Most programs operated by CIEE (Council on International Educational Exchange), for example, now offer a course called Seminar on Living and Learning Abroad, in which students discuss their experiences in the local culture and what they have observed about habits, expectations, and assumptions. Talking about your reflections with other people often opens new insights regarding your own cultural perspectives and new ideas about the motivations and values of the local population.

Strategy 8: Improve Your Language Abilities

One of the most important skills for living in another country and learning a different culture is to learn to communicate in the language. Many faculty and study abroad professionals will encourage you to learn as much language as you can before you go and certainly to pursue your language study while abroad. Although many people around the world do speak English, it is a sign of respect to learn as much as you can of their language, even if it is just "survival" words or phrases at first.

I know from personal experience the challenges of speaking a language. When I first arrived in Russia, I wanted so much to be able to listen, understand, and speak effectively with those I met. It was frustrating to hear words I didn't understand and to try to say things for which I lacked vocabulary. Spending more time studying, reading, and speaking made a big difference, and I found that the more I spoke and asked questions, the more I understood and the better I felt when talking with the locals. Later, as my own abilities improved and as I interacted with fellow U.S. Americans who visited Russia, I noticed that I understood more situations, caught more details, and appreciated the nuances of many situations better than they did. I realized how important the investment of time and effort in learning another language had been for me.

I am not pretending that learning a foreign language is easy. Far from it. Rather, I want to emphasize that learning a language takes time, patience, and a willingness to speak, even when you make mistakes. It takes hours of homework and practice. Language learning is like a muscle: The more you use it, the stronger it will become. I am always surprised at the number of students who think they will become "fluent" in a language in just one semester yet schedule trips outside their study abroad country on a regular basis. How can a person expect to learn a language when he or she does not invest the time and energy to do it?

Even in countries where English is the predominant language or at least one of the official languages, it is important to remember that there are numerous words and phrases that have meanings different from the meanings we expect in the United States. For example, although British English and American English are largely similar, there are numerous phrases used in Britain that have different meanings when said in the States. Many U.S. Americans have learned, to their chagrin, that it is best not to speak in public about wearing *pants*, which are normally worn underneath the clothing. It is *slacks* that men wear to work. Other examples of "false friends" and phrases that have differing meanings can be found in Australia, Canada, Ghana, Ireland, India, New Zealand, Nigeria, Hong Kong, and other places where English is widely spoken.

Strategy 9: Learn How to Learn Experientially

One of the critical skills for navigating another country or culture is to pay attention to details, watch how people speak and act, and adjust your own behavior where it seems appropriate. We call this ability to learn from one's experiences "experiential learning," and it is a key part of becoming a culture sleuth. When you get right down to it, this is something you have done all your life. So why discuss it here? Because experiential learning is something you can develop in other areas of life as well, not just when traveling abroad. In fact, paying attention to how people act and interact and looking for the meaning behind their words and actions are essential to being an effective employee and team member.

Perhaps the major aspect of experiential learning is to reflect on what you have seen or heard and discuss your reflections with others (see Strategy 7). In programs that have a service-learning focus, this reflection is often done through writing a journal or participating in group discussions. It is common for one person to notice certain things or to have different insights into certain experiences, so discussing things with others allows for sharing and comparing perspectives. There are many ways to reflect and to learn from others, even if you are the only student from your college or university at your study abroad program or host university.

Strategy 10: Have Fun!

Crossing into another culture can be enjoyable and eye-opening, especially if you establish a friendship that endures beyond the time in-country. Cross-cultural engagement can be fun because of the people you meet, the things you see, the places you visit, and the food you eat. The process can also be enriching because of the things you learn about yourself, the skills you develop, and the insights you gain into the diversity of the human experience. Studying abroad can help you gain self-confidence in your language abilities and experience the sheer joy of being able to communicate in new and different ways, despite the frustrations and potential embarrassment that occasionally accompany learning a new language.

Embrace these opportunities for personal growth and learning about other people, other countries, and other ways of looking at the world. Don't retreat from the chance to meet new people, hear their stories, and learn about what matters most to them. In the process, you'll be building bridges, changing perceptions, and creating understanding. Your work as an ambassador will help others understand you and your home country, while you help others understand the people and perspectives of your host country. In small yet significant ways, you will be changing the world.

3

VISIBLE DIMENSIONS
OF CULTURE
Food, Art, Clothing, Music, and Holidays

Profile 3: Heather Kraft

Studying abroad is one of the most beneficial decisions I have made. While furthering my cultural horizons, I also learned about myself in a manner that would not be possible without this type of experience.

Before I left for Madrid, I had not really realized the implications of going to another country, traveling alone, and living with a complete stranger for five weeks. Initially, I was not nervous or anxious but rather calm. It wasn't until I walked off the plane and into the Madrid airport that I realized I was completely on my own. Without an inexpensive way to communicate with people from home while traveling, I was forced to be independent and use as many resources as I could discover. I developed many different skills, such as language proficiency, time management, and coordination of activities. While these are not major changes, they are adaptations. I transformed into a more independent person. Most people think that going to college is a method of finding independence, but after studying abroad I have realized that placing oneself in a foreign country with no connections is the only true manner of finding independence. Being able to communicate with the locals is highly important so that you may ask for directions and advice and simply interact in day-to-day conversations.

What changed the most about me is my palate. I have always been a picky eater who would never try new things. When I went to Spain, this quickly changed. I lived with a host mother who cooked dinner for me on a daily basis. To be respectful, I always ate what was presented to me and cleaned my plate. I tried a variety of new foods, and this is one change

31

that has carried over into my current lifestyle now that I am back in the United States.

Another change that came from my study abroad experience is my sleeping habits and extracurricular activities. In Spain it is not uncommon to go out multiple nights of the week until late morning. This is something I was not accustomed to. I learned to take naps in the afternoon and experienced some nighttime activities that lasted until 8:00 a.m. In Spain there is a "siesta" in the afternoon sometime between 2:00 and 5:00 where people have time to go home from work and rest or relax. This is not a habit practiced in the United States, but it is something I got very used to. I had to get accustomed to the afternoon nap time in order to make it through the long nights that the Spaniards enjoy on a regular basis. While the siesta is a change that I have tried to incorporate into my daily lifestyle, staying out until late morning is a change I have resisted since being home. That habit often made me tired during the day, and my lifestyle in the United States is not something that can accommodate for such extracurricular activities.

Since I was abroad, my goals have dramatically changed. I now plan on pursuing a career in international business. I am very interested in working for a multicultural company or one with a global reach. I have also rediscovered my interest in the Spanish language. In the next five years, I plan to devote some time to relearning the language and hopefully incorporating it into my career.

The easiest way to begin your culture sleuthing and to find more ways to interact with the locals is to observe the many ways people in another culture live on a daily basis. You will find that they do things that are similar and different from the things you do. This chapter focuses on some of the visible dimensions of culture, or the outward expressions of what people do on a regular basis that may be shaped by their cultural values, norms, and expectations. In later chapters we will look at practices that require us to observe behavior, habits, and some inward dimensions of life to discover their cultural values. All cultures contain both outward expressions and inward behaviors, values, and expectations that go together, as predicted by the concept of culture as an iceberg (see Chapter 1).

The goal of exploring the visible aspects of other cultures is to try to uncover the values and expectations people have and to find common ground for personal interactions. This will help in your efforts to meet more of the locals and to step outside "the bubble" in authentic ways.

Food

Did you ever think that the food you eat and how you eat it reveals your own cultural values and practices? Think about it. Beyond the phrase "you are what you eat" (a phrase that encourages schoolchildren in the United States to pay attention to the foods they consume every day), what you eat reveals many things about your own culture. It reveals your cultural values regarding where you get your food, how it is prepared, how much time is taken to prepare it, who you eat meals with and in what settings, and much, much more. Obviously, the same is true of people in other countries.

We all have impressions of certain categories of foods and where they generally come from. For example, we might associate pasta and pizza with Italy, "Chinese food" with China, beans and tortillas and burritos with Mexico, and so on. But as we visit other countries, we generally find that those superficial associations are too simplistic. It is useful to begin thinking about the role of food and meals in a culture and what they reveal about the expectations people have regarding nutrition, food preparation, time with family and friends, and hospitality, among other things.

There are many ways to think about food and the habits and expectations that revolve around meals and food preparation. Let's begin with you. What time do you eat meals, and who is with you when you eat? Who prepares your meals, both at home and while you are at college? Many families in the United States eat dinner together, with parents, children, and perhaps grandparents sitting down at the table at the same time, often around 6:00 or 7:00 p.m. This traditional U.S. American meal has been glorified for many years, especially since the 1950s when television shows such as *The Adventures of Ozzie and Harriet* focused attention on the two-parent household. But this "sit-down" meal is not the norm for many other families, particularly when members of the family work shifts other than 9:00 to 5:00 or attend college or training programs. In many cases, members of such households eat at different times, sometimes at a dinner table, sometimes in front of the television or computer, and sometimes in a car or truck or "on the run."

Your own attitudes toward meals and mealtime are naturally shaped by your experiences growing up, as well as your preferences regarding meals while at college. This includes your own expectations for what utensils you use (fork only, fork with knife, chopsticks, etc.) and which hand you tend to eat with. In the United States, it is common to eat primarily with a fork in the right hand, only moving the fork to the left hand when cutting with a knife. In many countries it is common for people to hold a fork in the left hand and knife in the right hand for the entire meal. In parts of Asia, chopsticks are the norm. In other countries it is common for people to eat not with utensils but with their right hand out of a communal platter of food, together with family and friends. Meals are a group experience in many cultures.

How much do you talk when you eat a meal? In many U.S. American families, it is common for mealtime to be a time to connect with each other, to discuss what happened during the day, and so on. People may talk and eat at the same time, or they remain at the table for an extended period of time. Naturally, in such families the dinner table is treated as a warm, inviting place, a location where family members discuss life, work, school, challenges, relationships, and much more. Other families, on the other hand, spend little time talking during a meal. In such families, dinnertime is considered a time to relax and think, or even to pause from thinking, and discussions about life and work take place in other settings or at other times of the day, or perhaps not at all. In other families, individuals eat separately, perhaps while watching television, using the computer, reading the newspaper, or doing some other activity. There is similar variety of approaches to mealtimes abroad.

Holidays and celebrations reveal other aspects of our own cultural expectations regarding meals. It is fairly universal to celebrate key events in our history, such as Independence Day and days signifying political or military victories or milestones. What foods do you associate with July 4th, Memorial Day, and Labor Day? Because these events take place during the summer, many U.S. Americans associate these days with picnics, cookouts, or barbecues. You may also have family traditions on such days, such as going on a hike, playing a game of baseball, visiting a cemetery, swimming, and so on, that also revolve around meals and the people you are with. How about Christmas, Hanukkah, Cinco de Mayo, Carnaval,

Navruz, Ramadan, or New Year's? Do you have different food traditions for holidays or celebrations in the winter?

The foods you eat and the people you spend holidays with provide many insights into your own cultural practices, even though you might not think of it that way. Just ask five friends to list 10 to 20 foods and activities they associate with July 4th or another holiday, and you will likely find things that you all share in common, as well as things that are unique to each person. It is natural that people around the world have similar traditions and associate their own holidays with certain foods, activities, and people.

Natalie Duffy

Before going abroad, I would tend to eat extremely fast and often by myself—my family always attempted to have dinner together, but with numerous activities and work schedules, it was often difficult for us to organize that. When I was in Italy, dinner wasn't just a time to eat, it was a whole event. When we would eat dinner in Italy, my friends and I formed our own family and would often spend up to three hours eating, drinking wine, and sharing things about ourselves. In Italy, I would also eat much slower. Meals in Italy aren't just about feeding your body; they are an entire social event.

Next, let's turn to how food is prepared. In the United States it has become common to purchase premade meals that are frozen or stored in cans or jars. It is common to purchase meals in restaurants geared toward fast food, where the amount of time necessary to prepare a meal is minimal and where meals can be consumed quickly. Many in the United States rely on packaged foods such as chips, pretzels, crackers, and cookies that are prepared many miles away. Our focus on fast food and short meals not only has an impact on the nutritional content of our meals but also reveals our attitudes toward time and convenience, as well as the amount of time we spend with family or friends during meals. These expectations and trends are part of our culture.

By contrast, in many places around the world, food is prepared from raw ingredients ("from scratch") for almost every meal. In many cultures, people spend much more time preparing meals and sharing them with family and friends. In France, for example, it is common to shop daily for groceries, such as fresh bread, vegetables, and meat or fish. In some countries, there are fewer prepackaged foods, so meals are prepared from fresh ingredients out of necessity.

Another area of potential difference is the time of day when different meals are eaten. Students who study in Spain are often shocked at the lateness of lunch and dinner, which take place hours later than many U.S. Americans eat those meals. Some students adjust quickly to the new mealtimes, whereas others prefer to maintain their habits from home. They also discover that many Spaniards travel home for lunch and siesta and that many shops close for a couple hours because of this tradition.

This section on food and meals would be incomplete without mention of beverages, including alcohol. Many cultural traditions and habits related to what we drink, either with meals or on their own, stem from premodern times when it was difficult to find pure water. Coffee, tea, and other beverages are prepared with water that has been boiled in order to kill any nasty bugs. Beer and wine contain enzymes that kill bacteria and other things that could make a person sick. Consequently, such drinks became staples in the diet over hundreds of years. It is relatively easy to see the legacy of these age-old traditions today, including the attitudes and behaviors associated with alcohol. Beer and wine are routinely consumed as a part of lunch or dinner in many countries, and the food consumed with the alcohol reduces the likelihood of a person becoming intoxicated. Although drunkenness and alcoholism are certainly common in other cultures (I have seen many men and women in Russia and Finland who were plastered), it is considered bad behavior in many parts of the world to be intoxicated in public. In addition, alcohol abuse contributes to a large proportion of the injuries and emergencies that occur among study abroad students.

Behind all of these patterns relating to food, beverages, and meal traditions are numerous cultural values that shape attitudes and behaviors. Aside from keeping us alive, meals also demonstrate attitudes toward time with family and friends and the importance of various foods in the culture. Paying attention to such details and looking beyond the superficial can reveal much more about the culture and traditions than may be apparent on first glance. Being a culture sleuth means looking for patterns within food traditions that are both similar to and different from your own habits and preferences. You will likely discover foods and traditions that you really enjoy and may even miss after you return home.

Art, Dance, and Artistic Expression

Another area of life that is visible to the naked eye is art, dance, and other forms of artistic expression. (We'll discuss music in a later section.) Have you ever stopped to consider your own expectations and preferences regarding art? What types of dancing do you participate in, whether with family or friends or when you are alone? What types of art do you like, and how often do you paint, make a sculpture, or create objects using things like plaster, ceramic, or fabric? Do you sew, knit, or weave things someone can wear? Do you enjoy colorful objects, paintings, or posters? What types of objects do you have on display in your home or college housing? As with food, the traditions and behaviors associated with artistic expression are rooted in the past and provide valuable insights into the values and behaviors that are acceptable or encouraged in a culture. We need to keep in mind that a country may have multiple cultures, based on languages spoken, ethnic groups, economic or social classes, political ideology, religion, and many other things.

A useful way to begin learning about the arts that are valued in a culture is to identify the artists whose works appear in leading museums in the country where you will be studying. When many people think of culture, they often think of art, particularly the forms of painting, sculpture, and other art that appear in museums. These "high-culture" forms of art are wonderful accomplishments, and many people in your host country will expect that you know a bit about their accomplished artists. Set a goal for yourself to identify 5 to 10 artists whose work appears in a museum or national gallery in your host country and one or two pieces of art for which each one is recognized. Create this list before you leave for abroad. If you will be studying in Italy, for example, your list might include Renaissance artists such as Michelangelo, Raphael, or Leonardo da

Vinci or Baroque painters such as Caravaggio. If you will be studying in China, your list could include artists or artistic trends from
the Tang, Song, Yuan, Ming, or Qing dynasties. Learning about
major works, or even two or three categories or trends of such art
(e.g., religious, impressionist, expressionist, cubist), will give you a
starting place for understanding some key artistic accomplishments
in your host country. You will also have more to discuss with the
locals you meet, who will be impressed that you are taking time to
learn about their country and culture.

Of course, paintings are not the only items that appear in
museums or galleries. Sculptures are also impressive in terms of the
time, effort, and skill necessary to create them. Many museums also
include fabric art, clocks, jewels, and other items. The "Peacock
Clock," for example, is a central item in the Hermitage Museum
in St. Petersburg, Russia. Crowns, jewels, scepters, and other rega-
lia also appear in museums and galleries. The Internet now hosts
hundreds of articles and thousands (or millions) of images that will
speed up your investigation of majors works and artists. Ideally, your
study abroad program will schedule at least one visit to a museum
or gallery. If not, find a time to go on your own or with a friend.

Our conception of art and artistic expression does not need to
end (or begin) with museum-quality art. The world is filled with
other forms of art and artistic expression that we associate with popular culture. There are numerous artists who do high-quality work
that does not appear in museums. Just look around you, and you'll
find other examples, from the knickknacks you have in your own
room and items you have on your walls to what you see on television
or in the media. Professional sports teams, for example, use colors,
logos, and stylized figures to encourage attendance or to sell tickets,
posters, balls, and related paraphernalia. In Russia, it is common
for people to display Orthodox Christian icons, as well as stacking
dolls or jewelry boxes made from wood and painted with scenes
from the countryside. Such items may remind people of themes or
stories from their faith tradition or the history of their family, ethnic
group, or nation. The physical artifacts of popular culture will likely
be among the first things you notice when you arrive and the most
common souvenir items you take home with you.

Dance, likewise, extends beyond the theatrical performances seen in a theater. Dancing and rhythmic body movements are associated with celebrations and holidays in many parts of the world. If you have a chance to attend a ballet or dance performance in a theater, do it. If you enjoy participating in any form of dance, such as ballet, ballroom, tap, or modern, find a club or group that you can join, even for a few weeks. Although many study abroad programs do not automatically sign students up for local clubs, virtually all of the on-site study abroad staff I have met over the years have been eager to help students join a local club that matches their interests. Those students who do take advantage of such clubs have reported that the time they spent doing this has opened doors to friendships, discussions, and opportunities to practice their language. These interactions often become highlights of their time abroad.

Holidays and cultural celebrations provide students additional opportunities to watch or participate in dance and music in another culture. Students who study in New Zealand, for example, often attend a traditional Māori dance, such as the Haka, or participate in cultural celebration. Students who study in Africa enjoy the many forms of participatory dance that are key parts of local celebrations. Those studying in Spain, Italy, Greece, and many parts of Latin America should take advantage of opportunities to try their hand (and feet) in the many forms of folk dances, such as flamenco, salsa, and tango. Learning about such dances and the role of dance in the culture will reveal new insights about your hosts. It will create additional opportunities to form friendships, get outside the bubble, and engage in the local culture. As a culture sleuth, pay attention to details regarding when and where different dances are performed and who participates in them. You may want to teach your family and friends some of the new dances that you learn while abroad.

Clothing

Another area of life that reveals attitudes toward color and art is clothing. What are your attitudes toward the clothes you wear? How much time do you spend each day thinking about your clothing and outfits and how you will wear them, including any jewelry, makeup, scarves, or belts you'll include? How often do you wear jeans or shorts? How much skin on your arms, legs, and chest can be seen when you wear your favorite clothes? Do you find yourself thinking or talking about the clothes your friends, parents, siblings, and neighbors wear? What kinds of shoes or footwear do you prefer? Do you realize that your clothing and style reveal significant things about your culture and cultural values?

Many aspects of clothing reveal what is valued in a country or culture. For example, in the United States we value our independence. This shows up in a variety of ways in our clothing, from the wide variety of clothing worn to the words and logos printed on many T-shirts. It shows up in the amount of skin many people are willing to show when wearing shorts, shirts, skirts, blouses, and dresses. Other cultures are more traditional when it comes to the way people dress. Muslim cultures, for example, expect women to cover much of the skin as a basic tenet of their beliefs. As a result, most Muslim women expose only their face, hands, and ankles when out in public. In many Christian communities, women enter a church building only if they wear a dress or skirt and a head scarf. Jewish communities likewise embrace different styles of clothing, including a head covering. In many of these cultures, it is uncommon for women and men to wear shorts in public or for women to reveal cleavage. The clothing people wear is very much shaped by cultural attitudes and norms.

Another aspect of the way people dress relates to style. Many U.S. American women who study in France, Italy, and Spain, for example, notice how strong the fashion sense is and how stylish people appear in public. Many people have remarked over the years that French women must have a gene for using scarves and belts to make any outfit look stylish and classy. Being well dressed and stylish is important in China, Japan, and many other countries in Asia as well, although the preferred styles and fashions may differ from those in Europe.

Shoes and footwear is another area of clothing that deserves attention. In the United States, it is common for men and women to wear sneakers or "tennis shoes" throughout the day. It is less common for people to wear sneakers in other countries, where men wear black or brown dress shoes and women wear pumps or heels.

U.S. Americans visiting other countries can often be identified more quickly by what they wear on their feet, including the color and styles of socks, than by the clothing they wear. As a culture sleuth, pay attention to footwear and what men, women, and children wear at different times of day.

Study abroad students generally don't have the time or money to study the local styles or replace their entire wardrobe in the course of a few short weeks or months. Most study abroad advisors recommend that you pack light and take fewer items of clothing with you when going abroad. This will allow you to purchase a few items of clothing abroad once you have time to determine how the weather and culture affect what people wear at certain times of the year and find your own way to blend in. This gives you the chance to imitate the local style or pick up slacks, blouses, saris, or other common items of clothing.

As you prepare to study abroad, spend some time thinking about what types of clothing are widely accepted in the country or countries where you will be traveling. Ask returned study abroad students who have been to that country not only for recommendations of what to wear but for descriptions of what the locals wear at different times of year. Some websites have useful information regarding the clothing people wear, but it is often best to talk with knowledgeable people who have lived in-country for a few months. If you will be visiting other countries during your time abroad, ask detailed questions about the places you will be visiting. Certain things will mark you as being a tourist or a U.S. American, but you will blend in better if you avoid common pitfalls, such as wearing T-shirts emblazoned with text or wearing shorts when few of the locals do. Keep in mind that the seasons will be different in the southern hemisphere.

If you are unsure about what clothing to take with you when going abroad, don't panic. Pack a variety of some items you have learned through your research might help you blend in. Pack light, and give yourself a week or two to observe what people wear, then purchase one or two inexpensive items that will help you fit in with those around you. Standing out like a sore thumb can be annoying personally and can also make you more of a target for pickpockets.

Music

What role does music play in your life and the lives of your family and friends? Do you associate different kinds of music with different events or activities? Do you listen to music throughout the day (when you are not in class, that is) or just at certain times? What does the music you listen to reveal about your own traditions, religious beliefs, and upbringing? Have you noticed that you prefer different types of music than others around you do, or do you find yourself listening to and enjoying the same songs as your friends and neighbors?

Just as people in the United States like a variety of music, from rock, rap, and R&B to soul, country, and classical orchestral, people who live in other countries also enjoy a variety of musical traditions. While abroad you may even hear recent English-language songs in public places such as malls, where business owners try to draw in those who want to be "hip" by listening to the latest U.S. American or British stars. But what do you know of more traditional forms of music in the country where you will be studying?

As with clothing styles and art, you can also do some research on the types of music that are common to your study abroad host country. Identify at least three to five well-known artists or genres of music. For example, if you will be studying in India, use Wikipedia or other online resources to find out about the region's classical music traditions, such as Carnatic and folk music. Then learn about more recent trends, such as Indi-pop and hip-hop. Likewise, if you will be studying in China, learn about traditional Chinese music and musical forms, as well as more recent trends and artists. In countries large and small, you will find regional variations and traditions associated with different language or ethnic groups.

Other important aspects of music include the words and stories they contain, as well as when and where they are played or performed. You probably recognize certain songs or hymns that you would associate with weddings and religious services, as well as independence day celebrations and funerals. The same will be true in your study abroad country, though the songs and hymns will be different. It is valuable to consider what types of messages are being communicated through music. Do different songs or types of music serve to inspire patriotism or help people to mourn, for example? Your cultural sleuthing includes paying attention to more subtle details in the music you hear while abroad.

Holidays

Music, clothing, and art are often associated with holidays and celebrations. For example, what types of music do you hear on your favorite holiday? Do you dress differently on that day? What types of foods do you associate with July 4th, Memorial Day, Labor Day, or New Year's? What kinds of traditions does your family follow on those days? Do you have wonderful memories of holidays and traditions in your family? Or do you associate difficult or painful memories with certain holidays because of events in the past? Does your family celebrate religious holidays, such as Epiphany, Rosh Hashanah, Ramadan, Easter, or Christian saints' days? Or do you generally mark only those holidays identified by government, such as Labor Day? Do you celebrate the New Year on a day other than January 1st?

Your own past and experience regarding holidays shape what you expect others will do during their holidays. For example, many students experience Memorial Day as a day off from work or a day to sleep in, whereas others celebrate the day by attending or participating in a parade or memorial service at a church, cemetery, or school. Some families gather together for a picnic or party or travel to the beach or the mountains, whereas others spend the day at home or in front of a television or computer. In other words, many of us have our own traditions for certain holidays.

You may be surprised that people in other countries have other traditions or associate certain annual events with religious or ethnic celebrations. Students who study in Thailand, for example, will recognize the influence of Buddhism in the many holidays and celebrations, including the Thai New Year. Students who study in Barcelona will notice that many celebrations throughout Catalonia have a Christian history and are often used to emphasize Catalan traditions and identity. The examples go on and on.

You can learn more about the holidays and traditions in your study abroad country by identifying three to five holidays that are celebrated there. Find out what the locals do on that day, including the foods they eat, dances or music that are commonly performed, and any parades or gatherings that are commonly held. Include any religious or political aspects or overtones in your research. As you do this, you are preparing yourself for your study abroad experience and for interaction with your hosts. Your awareness of holidays and traditions will make you a better culture sleuth, and you will be better prepared for opportunities to discuss these things with the people you meet.

4

VISIBLE DIMENSIONS OF CULTURE

Infrastructure, Technology, and Shopping

Profile 4: Lauren Hull

Any cliché that people use to describe their study abroad experience could accurately describe my semester in Cameroon. It truly pushed me to be more open-minded, take a more global perspective, and examine a lot of my beliefs and preconceptions. Having the opportunity to stay in families' homes in the country and to be engaged in the various communities that I was a part of, in such a tangible way, allowed me to really begin to understand a culture and social class so different than what I've experienced before. The lifestyles of my host families there served as windows into the lives of people all over the world who live in developing countries and who far outnumber those living in what I have previously considered a pretty "normal" American lifestyle.

My perception of poverty totally changed. I was able to see that poverty is a very relative concept. While I often think of myself as "poor" among some of my peers in college, I have always been well provided for in essentially every area of my life. Likewise, many of the families I stayed with didn't see themselves as poor because they had a house of sorts and were always able to provide some level of daily food and clothes to their children. After living with them for just a week or so, even I began to see this standard of living as normal. Things that I might have originally been shocked by or uncomfortable with (like bucket showers, lack of refrigeration, beverages sold in used bottles, or hole toilets) now simply seemed practical. While I was recognizing the practicality of certain differences and even the environmental benefits to such differences, I also had to recognize that some of these differences represent huge gaps in education or the ability to provide. For example, the fact that none of my families could afford or thought it necessary to drink clean water was really troubling. Something that we get on soapboxes about in the United States and use to speak to people's consciences here is just daily life for a middle-class family in Cameroon.

While abroad, I also saw more clearly the perception of the United States and Americans held by people outside the country, and I could also better see what I think about the American identity and our ideals by comparing them with those of a nation very different from most Western cultures. I questioned our ideals of individuality and independence, our conceptions of family, of government, and of love. Seeing such different lifestyles lived out before my eyes and being a part of it forced me to rethink a lot of biases I didn't even know that I had. And honestly, I would still say that's where I am. My semester in Cameroon was an opportunity for exploration, but it was also a learning experience in how to explore and question. I discovered a culture and society so much more complex than I could begin to understand that I left with more questions about how to approach development than I came with. In so many areas of my life, whether it's my goals for the future and how I want to be involved with development projects looking forward or my perception of feminism and how I see the roles of husband and wife, I'm questioning previous ideas and continuing to explore what I currently believe. Learning from international friends coming from other cultures with different views on these topics has proved to be a really challenging and rewarding method for developing new and more nuanced perspectives, and I plan to continue searching out opportunities for this type of growth through friendships, travel, and education.

Cross-cultural engagement implies interaction with the people in your host country. As Lauren found (Profile 4), those interactions can give you a much better understanding of the values, habits, and expectations of your hosts. What may seem strange or odd from a U.S. American perspective can seem normal or typical when viewed from a different perspective.

In Chapter 3, we discussed some ways in which food, art, dance, clothing, music, and holidays offer windows into the cultural values, patterns, and expectations of the local population. These items give valuable information about the culture and what is valued by the people. This chapter focuses on other areas of life that are visible to the naked eye but that are often different from what you may be used to. Although the transportation networks, technology, and shopping processes may appear similar to what is present in your home community, many study abroad students are shocked to learn that there are different attitudes and expectations in other countries. Paying attention to how these areas function and asking questions regularly will help you be a better culture sleuth and will help you deal with the challenges that often arise in daily living abroad.

Buildings, Infrastructure, and Transportation

Although some may not think that buildings and infrastructure are part of a culture, our attitudes and expectations toward them are certainly part of our daily lives. For example, what types of buildings do you associate with the city or town where you live? Are you most comfortable in a large city, suburb, or small community? Are you comfortable in older buildings, or do you prefer only newly constructed homes, schools, community centers, and malls? What types of roads and transportation do you expect around you? Do you ride the bus, subway, train, or another form of public transportation on a regular basis? Or have you relied on your family's vehicles exclusively to this point in your life? Have you ever tried walking everywhere you need to go?

Many study abroad students find that navigating the transportation and infrastructure of another country can be among the most frustrating yet rewarding aspects of studying abroad. For example, a student from a suburb who has never ridden a bus or subway and then goes to Madrid, London, Paris, Berlin, Tokyo, or any other large city may feel overwhelmed at first in learning how to get from Point A to Point B. Learning how the local transportation systems work can feel like a daunting task at first, and many travelers rely on small charts or maps to navigate the different bus, subway, tram, and train lines and figure out how the price structure works. After living in such a city for a semester, however, such students develop a certain pride in being able to travel with confidence across a large city, picking the right bus or train line, and leading visitors to

destinations across town. Other students study in a rural community or less developed location, where buses or public transit may
be limited or even primitive. Finding a safe bus or van for intercity
travel can take hours in many parts of the world. Regardless of the
program location, many students find that learning how to overcome the frustrations and fears of transportation to be among their
most rewarding accomplishments while abroad.

Have you ever stopped to ask yourself what the citizens in
your study abroad country think about their own transportation
and infrastructure? What do they expect their own government
and community will provide in terms of public transportation and
infrastructure, and how might their expectations be different or
similar to your expectations of your own community? In many
European cities, for example, separate bicycle lanes and paths are
now common, and many locals prefer the "green" element of riding
a bike or walking to be liberating. In other communities, people
enjoy extensive networks of trams, buses, trolleys, and trains that
travel frequently and "on time" around a big city. They often interpret their transportation network as a sign of a civilized or advanced
society, taking pride in these aspects in their community.

In other cities and communities, and particularly in less developed parts of the world, the local transportation networks may
seem chaotic and poorly organized. Narrow city streets may be
shared by large buses and trucks, individual cars and taxis, and
motorbikes, as well as bikes, hand-push trolleys, and even animals.
It may seem like a "free for all" atmosphere on the roads, where the
largest or fastest vehicle has the right of way. Getting from Point
A to Point B may be challenging, and buses, whether privately or
publicly funded, may have irregular schedules and erratic routes.
People from more developed parts of the world often point to the
chaotic transportation and infrastructure as evidence of cultural
backwardness or government inaction and adopt an attitude of cultural superiority. They often forget that many developed countries
had weak infrastructure even a few decades ago. In other words,
such attitudes of cultural superiority are frequently misguided
because they miss the big picture of what is going on within a society and its economy.

As you prepare for your study abroad experience, do some research on the transportation networks in your study abroad country and the places you plan to visit. Find out how the systems work, how and where one should pay for services, and what the rules and expectations are for riding public transit. Are you expected to pay in cash at the front of the bus each time? Will you be expected to have exact change for each ride, or will the driver or money collector be able (and willing) to give change? Is it possible to buy a monthly pass or electronic card, such as London's Oyster Card or the Barcelona Transport Card, so you can easily pay for transit on any train, subway car, tram, or bus? Operating procedures tend to differ from one city or region to the next, much like the subway systems in New York City and Washington, DC, use different equipment, pricing, and schedules. You still may be surprised by certain aspects of transportation, such as where to find signs, but you will be better prepared if you do some research in advance.

In addition to learning about ticket prices, you should also pay attention to how people act when they wait for, board, and exit public transportation. Do they line up in an orderly manner (as in Tokyo) or rush forward as quickly as possible? Are you expected to signal to a bus driver that you would like to get on a bus? Do people need to stamp or validate a travel ticket upon entering a bus? Are seats reserved for women, children, older people, or those with disabilities? Once inside a bus or train, are riders expected to push a button or pull a cord to alert the driver that they wish to get out? What words do people say to each other when getting off? In St. Petersburg, Russia, I learned that people on subways move toward the door while the train is still moving, then ask the people in front of them something like "Are you here?" This phrase was shorthand for "Are you getting off here?" but at first it was very confusing to me what they were asking and what kind of response they expected. I learned that I should say "yes" or "no" to others and that I should also ask the same question when I wanted to get off but could not tell whether others closer to the door were getting off at the next stop or simply standing in that space.

A group of Wake Forest students in Dublin were shocked when the bus they were waiting for never stopped to pick them up at the bus stop where they had been standing for nearly one hour. They later learned that people waiting for a bus at a designated bus stop should watch for their intended bus number, then hold out their arm to signal the driver to stop for them. After this frustrating experience, they observed how the locals acted at the bus stop and learned to imitate their actions.

One area of infrastructure that many people take for granted is water and sewer service, in particular the availability of hot, running water. It is common for many U.S. Americans to take a hot shower on a daily basis, often lasting 20 to 30 minutes at a time. Attitudes toward both showers and cleanliness, as well as the use or conservation of water, are often different in other countries. For example, many people in Europe keep showers short (4 to 5 minutes) in order to conserve water, even though hot water may be available throughout the day. They may also go several days between showers. Students in home stays report being shocked when a host parent asks them to keep their showers to 5 minutes or less and perhaps more shocked to learn that people might not shower on a daily basis. In other countries, hot water may be available only periodically, so people develop other patterns and strategies for showering or bathing. For example, when I lived with a family in Russia several years ago, there was a month in the summer when hot water was out for the entire neighborhood, so the family boiled hot water that I poured over my head out of a bucket. This was a different type of shower, but it accomplished my goal. Lauren, the student who wrote the profile at the start of this chapter, found that showering out of a bucket is common in Cameroon. Expectations regarding water usage vary from country to country and from region to region.

Jim Kavalec

My time spent in Italy has changed my personal values. Although there is a strong green movement in the United States, our efforts are tame compared to those of Italy. The Italians have separate containers for glass, metal, and plastic instead of one container for all three. If one resident does not dispose of any of these items properly, the entire block receives a fine. In addition to this, lights are never kept on, even in public buildings, such as universities. Italians also use much smaller hot water tanks, so water conservation is always essential. After I lived with these constrictions for four months, it now feels unnatural for me to not practice green habits, and I have embraced the movement. Prior to leaving, recycling and saving energy and water never crossed my mind.

Another aspect of infrastructure is the trash collection system, including how, when, and where refuse is picked up and taken to a dump or collection point and how much used paper, glass, metal, and plastic is recycled. Study abroad students who have a habit of recycling are often surprised at how little is recycled in certain countries or by the seemingly cavalier attitudes of the locals. Other students find that the "reduce, reuse, recycle" approach to life has been more widely adopted in certain cities than in their own hometown. They might get yelled at if they try to put glass or plastic in a trash can rather than in a recycling bin because local expectations and assumptions are different from their own.

Beyond public transportation, try to become informed about other aspects of your host country's infrastructure, such as the trash system, electrical networks, and telephone and Internet providers. Knowing even a little about such systems will make you a better informed visitor. Once you arrive in-country, be sure to pay attention to how others act. Whether you live in an apartment, dormitory, or home stay, observe what people in your building or neighborhood do on a daily basis, and ask questions if something seems different or strange to you. Observe the local habits and expectations. Your role as a culture sleuth continues throughout the day.

The Role of Technology

Transportation, buildings, and infrastructure become part of a culture because of the habits and expectations people have about them. In addition, people around the world also have expectations regarding technology generally. This is true in developed countries and in developing countries. As with other aspects of culture, the habits, norms, and expectations you have regarding technology do change over time, albeit gradually. Culture sleuths look for both similarities and differences between their own habits and expectations about technology and the habits and expectations of people in other countries.

The cell phone is one form of technology that has evolved substantially and shaped our habits and expectations. Just a generation or two ago, few people carried a cell phone, and those who did have a portable phone found them cumbersome. In just a few years, cellular technologies changed dramatically both in the United States and around the world, and billions of cell phones are now in use. In the United States, many have come to expect that cellular service is quick, reliable, and relatively inexpensive compared with landline telephones. Many also expect that the companies that support these networks provide immediate customer service "with a smile." Have you ever stopped to think about what you would do without your smart phone, easy access to Facebook, or any of the other electronic devices that are part of your daily life?

Cellular and digital technologies are rapidly changing the way individuals, groups, and families communicate and the habits they have regarding communication. However, this technological change has been more extensive in some areas and less impactful in other areas. In most big cities, cellular service is now widespread and fairly reliable, although the actual technologies vary. In contrast, in many rural areas cellular service is limited or nonexistent, and this can be frustrating to someone who has become accustomed to 24/7 access to cell phones.

Other forms of technology that are changing rapidly include television, radio, and access to music and entertainment. Just a generation ago, many people watched television programs and set their daily schedules around this form of entertainment so they could watch specific programs that were shown only once. With the rise of digital media, it is now increasingly common for people to access old and new shows on their own schedule and in a variety of forms and locations. As these changes have occurred, cultural expectations about entertainment, media, technology, and easy access to multiple forms of entertainment are also changing.

As a culture sleuth, you have the task to observe the way others use technology and to discover their attitudes toward these devices and equipment. You may discover that teenagers and young adults in your host country are just as connected and dependent on new technologies as you are, although they may interact with their devices and each other differently than you do. You may also find that the locals place a lower value on having the latest gadgets and a greater value on relationships and speaking with others in person.

In developing parts of the world, where infrastructure is less developed, you may find that people are comfortable doing things the way their families have done them for decades or centuries. Your attitudes of being connected using the latest (and expensive) technologies may seem just as foreign to them as their comfort with older technologies is to you. In other parts of the world, you may find that the role of technology in daily life is changing more rapidly than in your hometown. Keep in mind that although people abroad may be using similar devices, their expectations of how and when they use them may differ from your own expectations.

Shopping

This section on visible cultural differences would be incomplete without a brief discussion about how and where we shop and what we expect from ourselves and others when we wish to purchase food, clothing, or other items. Many study abroad students expect that everything they find convenient in their home community will be readily available abroad. They are often shocked to find that habits and expectations are different in other locations. They find variations regarding when shops are open or closed, how items are arranged in shops, how customers are expected to act when shopping, and how those working at a store interact with customers. As you might expect, the "customer service" expectations we have in the United States differ from the patterns in other countries. Study abroad students are often shocked to learn that stores in some countries close in the middle of the day (such as Spain or Italy), that they close at 5:00 or 6:00, and that stores can seem small or cramped.

The following two student stories illustrate the shock or surprise that can occur when students begin to shop abroad and are not expecting any differences in the experience.

Natalie Duffy

One of my first weeks in Florence, I went to the grocery store to purchase some apples. I picked one up with my bare hand to make sure that it didn't have any bruises, and the next thing I knew an employee was coming at me, screaming in Italian. I had no idea what I was doing wrong, and it took a few minutes of me being reprimanded in Italian before I understood that I was supposed to be wearing a glove when handling fruit. The language barrier and difference in social customs were frustrating in this instance.

Jasmine Harris

When I first arrived in Ireland, my friends and I ate a lot of fast food because of its ready availability and its convenience; however, we later decided to go to the grocery store and buy real food. We walked about 20 minutes to a shopping center called the Omni in which there was a grocery store called Tesco. Tesco was the Irish equivalent of Walmart in that it was very large, and the food there was relatively cheap compared to other grocery stores. To shop for groceries, one of my friends used a Euro coin to release one basket from all the others, and we began to shop. We all went our separate ways in order to seek out the foods we wanted to purchase. As an individual with minimal cooking experience, I did not want to be too ambitious, so I sought out foods that I thought would be the easiest to prepare. I went straight to the frozen food aisle, but I had a lot of difficulty identifying what certain products were. Likewise, in other aisles of the store I found difficulty in trying to locate the foods that were on my list. I recognized that things weren't organized the way they would have been if I'd been in an American store. Also, many foods were called by a different brand name than they would have been in the United States; for example, Frosted Flakes were called Frosties. Some foods were called by completely different names: Chips were called "crisps," and fries were called "chips."

When I decided to check out, I had only a few of the items I intended to buy and others still that seemed like foods I would enjoy. In checking out I put my things on the conveyor belt and the cashier moved very quickly. The whole process was rushed not only because I had to pay but also because I had to almost simultaneously bag my own groceries. In addition, I was charged for the use of the plastic grocery bags. While making the 20-minute trek home, my friends and I realized we'd bought way too much food to carry such a long distance.

One word that would describe how I felt would be *overwhelmed*. The size of the grocery store and the way it was organized was a bit intimidating. Also, feeling as if I was rushed during the checkout added to this feeling. I also felt frustrated as I tried to find items that I felt were placed in an illogical fashion. The most frustrating thing was trying to find soup because the soup aisle was largely composed of baked beans. It was also difficult finding frozen food because there were two frozen food sections at opposite ends of the store. I also found it a bit irritating to have to carry all the groceries back to campus.

I know I felt the way I did because I'm used to knowing exactly what's going on, and in that situation I felt very much like a chicken with its head cut off. I was trying desperately to find my way but to no avail. I mistakenly made the assumption that the store would be organized exactly the same way an American store would, so by viewing the store through my own cultural lens, I became aggravated when differences occurred. I think I experienced culture shock because I believed in similarities that did not exist. The assumptions were made by the store owners that most Irish people would think that certain items should be on certain aisles; to them it made perfect sense, whereas to me it made none.

One of the most important intercultural skills I learned was the ability to anticipate differences. In going to Ireland, at times I felt the culture was very similar to that of the United States because on the surface it is very similar. However, I had to remind myself that differences did exist, and if I wasn't careful to take note of that, I could potentially end up in a similarly trying situation.

As a culture sleuth, you need to pay attention to details and observe the actions of others. For example, noticing how other customers carry their items (in shopping carts, in their hands, or in a carrying pouch), what they do when presenting their items to the shop clerk (putting items on a conveyor or handing them directly to the clerk), how they pay (using cash or credit cards, how they present money to the clerk), what they say during the interaction, and how they carry or pack up the items purchased (in plastic bags or shopping bags they brought to the store or in plastic bags they purchase) offers valuable information about what is expected in the local context. The whole experience can feel frustrating at first, yet it is useful to know that the locals survive this process every day.

Shopping at local markets or shops where prices are not listed can be an experience unto itself. It is common around the world for people to negotiate the price of fruits and vegetables and meat, as well as such items as clothing, silk, and pearls and other jewelry.

These kinds of shopping experiences offer great opportunities to practice your language and cultural abilities and to observe the locals in action. At times it is essential to simply walk away from certain shopkeepers or people who want to sell you a cheap watch. However, the negotiation process in itself provides glimpses into the lives of local people (and often immigrants to your host country) that we don't regularly find in the middle of big cities or college campuses.

For me the main point is to learn from variations in shopping experiences. Although some study abroad students are shocked or dismayed about the different approaches to shopping and might feel tempted to ask, "How can these people live this way?" it is useful to step back and look for meaning in the similarities and differences between your own expectations and those you find abroad. Rather than feeling judgmental about the differences, you will find it useful to reflect on the patterns and historical reasons why certain things are done or why people act the way they do.

This chapter has focused on infrastructure, technology, and shopping, which are just a few of the many aspects of life abroad where we can notice differences between your life at home and life abroad. As noted previously, I recommend avoiding the tendency to consider your own way of living to be superior to how things are done in other countries. Looking for similarities and differences provides a glimpse into the values, behaviors, and expectations that have developed in other cultures. As a culture sleuth, you will pay attention to details of how transportation works, how people use technology, and how they act when shopping. Then you will try to adapt your behavior to match the local environment. It is useful to talk with your program director or study abroad program staff about your experiences, compare notes with other students, and look for patterns in how things work. As you become more experienced with noticing how visible aspects of culture work, you will be ready to look for details in the less visible aspects of daily life abroad.

5

LESS VISIBLE ELEMENTS
OF CULTURE

Relationships

Profile 5: Mark Huffman

As I take time to reflect over the past year, I find myself remembering all the great memories I experienced both here and overseas. While I understand that all my memories are special for their own unique reasons, there is one memory that I will cherish more than all the others. The special thing about this memory is that there are so many memories intertwined within this one. That memory was my decision to not only study abroad in Barcelona but also live in a home stay while I was there. Because of those decisions, I not only had an amazing time but also was able to change and grow as a person for the better.

As a person, I'd say studying abroad changed my personality completely. Whether it was my level of maturity or the way I viewed the world, my time in Barcelona taught me how to be independent and perceive the world in a more sophisticated way. Furthermore, I grew as an individual because I strove to push my boundaries and made an effort to go out of my comfort zone in order to understand another culture. This helped me grow as a person because it taught me to be more adaptable when dealing with people from different cultures, races, or ethnicities.

Although there were many challenges that helped me grow as a person while I was abroad, there were also a few that I avoided as well. In other words, while I was abroad, I saw other members in my group changing for all the wrong reasons. Rather than immersing themselves in the culture or taking the time to appreciate their situation, some students simply saw the experience as an opportunity to succumb to the many temptations of nightlife in Barcelona. I will not sit here and be a hypocrite, but the truth of the matter is that some did not see the line nearly as well as others. More than anything, this was frustrating to see because there were so many amazing opportunities in front of us that some individuals did not take the time to enjoy.

While my time abroad taught me a lot about myself, the most important change I made was my ability to adapt to living in a home stay with another family. Although this does not have one defining characteristic that I adapted, the overall experience taught me a lot about who I was as a person. Not only did I learn how to adapt to several challenging variables, but also I was amazed to see how total strangers could put so much responsibility and trust in me to help the household stay intact. This was particularly special to me because it was nice to feel like such an important asset to the family. Living in a home with no male presence besides myself, it was interesting to see how my Spanish mother trusted me with so many responsibilities without knowing me that well as an individual. This helped me mature because it gave me a better perspective toward the "bigger picture" in life. This is not to say that I was not relatively mature before my experience, but this particular opportunity allowed me to have a better respect for life as a whole.

Looking to the future, I hope to apply my experiences abroad to the bigger picture. Whether that will overlap with my future employment or simply at home with my family, the things I learned abroad will go a long way toward helping me grow and succeed as a person. To further expand my intercultural competence, I think it would behoove me to spend more time traveling in the future and to attend more cultural activities at school and in my community. Not only is this important for me to learn more about myself, but also practicing these habits will benefit me in future careers as well. However, despite all the benefits that these future experiences will bring me, the most important thing is that I will continue to participate in these activities because I enjoy the experiences. Although I studied abroad to experience something new and memorable, the aftermath has shown me that there was much more to the experience than I originally expected. Whether I grew as a person or challenged myself to be open-minded, I am happy with all the decisions I made as an individual. As I continue on my life journey in the years after Wake Forest, I will be able to apply everything I learned both on campus and overseas to this greater picture. Although studying abroad is only one of several great experiences I will have in my lifetime, I will cherish these memories and remember the many lessons I learned forever.

As you prepare to study abroad and as you arrive at your program, there are elements of culture that are harder to see than the art, music, transportation networks, and infrastructure. These elements of culture are difficult to see with our eyes, because they require observing the people and noticing differences and similarities in how they think and act. Interacting with the locals is necessary in order to understand the motivations, values, and assumptions that shape their behaviors and attitudes. We can think of these elements of culture as being parts of an iceberg below the waterline. They directly affect the more visible aspects of daily life that we have already discussed.

As you begin to interact with the locals while abroad, you will likely find that groups of people act differently depending on their age, occupation, gender, status, and so on. The same is true, of course, in whatever community you grew up in. It is highly unlikely that all people will be motivated by the exact same set of values as everyone else. In other words, there are "subcultures" or groups that act differently than others, and there can be generational differences as well. Individuals also have their own learning and communication style preferences, so sometimes it is hard to identify which behaviors are shaped by deeply held values and which are motivated by personality or personal preference.

Despite the existence of subgroups and subcultures, it is essential to look for the broad values or traits that are shared by large segments of the population, as well as the values and behaviors expected by various subgroups. For example, in the United States we highly value personal independence. This is a broad value that shapes how many, perhaps most, U.S. Americans act and believe, and it affects most subgroups as well. There are numerous examples of how U.S. Americans act that illustrate this strong sense of independence, from how we think about health care and public transportation to gun rights and government regulation. This widely held value of personal independence also shapes the attitudes of various subgroups in our society, ranging from video gamers to abortion rights advocates and opponents. The instinct to emphasize the right for a person to choose his or her actions in our country is strong in virtually every sphere of life. This instinct is less strong in many parts of the world, where choices are often shaped more by the needs of the group rather than by those of the individual.

Of course, we should not forget that there are many communities within the United States made up of immigrants from other countries who arrive with the cultural values and beliefs from their home country. If their home culture emphasized more group cohesion and attention to the needs of the family or group, they may be shocked by the widespread adherence to personal choice and independence in the United States. In addition, there are also many individuals and families in the United States that are more group or family oriented with less emphasis on personal preference. In other words, if your instincts toward personal independence are not as strong as those of your friends and classmates, and you feel that your actions and behaviors should be adjusted to the needs of your group or community, that is a reflection of how you operate according to a different set of cultural values, expectations, and beliefs.

Relationships

Let us begin with a fairly broad topic: relationships. Think of the various relationships that you have with the many individuals in your life, from parents and family members to friends, members of a team or club, roommates, classmates, professors and instructors, people you work with or meet in a work environment, your study abroad advisor, and so on. Whether you realize it or not, the relationships you form with these different people vary in their closeness and intensity. You probably treat them differently depending on their age and status, as well as the type of interaction expected. For example, as a college freshman you probably addressed your instructors as "professor" or "doctor" and approached them humbly or with caution, whereas the students in your residence hall or apartment saw a different side of you. You have probably paused more than once to ensure that your actions and words toward one person were in keeping with the type of relationship you already had or wanted to have with that person. You wouldn't want to talk the same way to your professors the way you talk with your best friends or that "special someone."

Similarly, you can expect that people who live in your study abroad country will know instinctively that relationships vary depending on one's familiarity or closeness to other people, as well as whether they are members of one's family or social group. What you may not expect is that the "rules" for how relationships are formed in your study abroad country may differ from the way relationships function where you live. In China, for example, the expectations of how parents and children treat each other will differ from those of people who live in Argentina, Germany, or Nepal.

As a culture sleuth, you have as one of your tasks to pay attention to how locals interact with each other, with you and other study abroad students, and with people visiting their country. At first it may seem obvious that they view you as an outsider or tourist, someone who is coming to enjoy their country and its resources for a short period of time but who has little interest in understanding the people. You can work to bridge that gap and overcome those perceptions through investing time and effort in learning the language, meeting the people, and trying to understand how they see the world.

The sections in this chapter and the next chapter explore a variety of dimensions of relationships, such as how an individual functions within a group, the nature of power and status within a society, and the role of gender and sexuality within the community. Naturally, these various elements affect how relationships are formed and expressed. Often, several elements of relationships are at play at the same time in other cultures, just as is the case in your own culture. As a culture sleuth, pay attention to a variety of details, such as the words people use when talking with others; their body language and actions while interacting; the age, status, and gender of those they are interacting with; and the emotions that are expressed during or after their interaction.

The Individual Within the Group

One of the areas where you can begin your observations abroad and develop your skills as a culture sleuth relates to how individuals function within their family, group, and society as a whole. Your own background and upbringing will affect how you do this, so be honest with yourself about your own expectations for how people and families (including your own) function.

As mentioned at the beginning of this chapter, many people in the United States have a strong impulse toward personal independence and choice. This is a cultural value that is reinforced by many people and in many ways. Researchers have concluded that this cultural value stems from the independence required hundreds of years ago in founding this country in a rugged and hostile environment and the process of settling new areas that later became the United States.

In other countries, the past may have shaped the importance of the family, one's religious group, or the community as the primary defense against poor harvests, adverse weather, war, and other external threats. Such factors have emphasized that being a contributing member in these societal groups may be more important to survival than individual choices that may leave the community divided or at risk. In other words, the past matters in how these countries and communities have formed and changed over time. In Russia, for example, a variety of factors contributed to the institution of the peasant community. Over hundreds of years, millions of Russian inhabitants relied on each other to survive against famine and bad weather, as well as to protect each other against their local masters during the time of serfdom. Although the institution of serfdom ended in Russia in the 1860s, the legacy of the peasant community lasted for decades and contributed to the creation of socialist communes during the Soviet Union. The combined legacy emphasized the importance of the community over personal independence as the means of surviving war, Soviet repression, and forced imprisonment or exile. Although Russian society continues to change since the collapse of the Soviet Union, the patterns of thinking about the importance of community continue on. Similar trends can be found from Africa to Asia and from Europe to Australia and Latin America.

In many countries, young people attend elementary and high school with almost the exact same set of children. They form tight bonds with their classmates through 8 to 12 years of being in school together. When these students arrive at college or university, it is no wonder that they prefer to spend time with the group of friends they have known for many years and may be less open to interact with a foreign student such as you who is visiting for just a few weeks. Being persistent in your efforts to interact with people in such cultures will still work, but it may take time. Joining a club and trying to speak their language will help you immensely in forming friendships in almost every case.

One area of life where relationships play a role is when a teenager or young adult selects a career. In many countries, the educational system separates young people into different tracks as early as middle school, placing those teenagers who seem appropriate for university or advanced training into one track and those slated for careers in industry or agriculture into other tracks. The pivotal decision about what type of training and career a person will have is therefore made fairly early, often when he or she is 14 or 15 years old and perhaps even younger. This type of educational "tracking" seems offensive to many U.S. Americans who carry a strong sense of personal independence and who believe people should have the right to choose their career and training later in life, despite how well they performed in middle school. In other countries, however, these tracking systems are viewed positively, as they allow scarce educational resources to be devoted to those who seem naturally more inclined to one area of work or skill. At its core, this type of educational system is favoring the needs of the group over the interests of the individual, as future engineers, doctors, and intellectuals are identified at a younger age and as society invests time and resources to prepare them for a life of service in the community.

Another fascinating area of relationships revolves around greetings, or how you greet people when you meet them. Think of what you do and say when you meet someone in one of the groups to which you belong. For example, when you meet one of your best friends, do you have a particular handshake you always use? Do you give a high five or greet each other with a kiss on the cheek? Do you say "hello" or "what's up"? What do you expect from these greetings? What kind of body language do you use for your close set of friends or family members? Do the rules for such interactions change for teachers or the school principal or dean?

In other countries, it is common for people to greet each other in particular ways, but the rules for such interactions will likely vary from what you expect. For example, in many cultures it is common to greet one's friends and family members with a kiss on the cheek. In some places, just one "air kiss" is expected. In other places, two or three kisses are expected to be given on different cheeks. Watch how people greet each other in your host country, and try to identify the rules for different types of interactions. For example, do young women of the same age follow the same pattern in greetings as when a younger woman meets an older woman? Do young adult men follow the same pattern as young adult women? Do the rules for such greetings change if someone is married or single? Do people expect you, as an outsider (at least at first), to follow the same pattern for greetings? How do these interactions change when people say good-bye or "take leave" of each other? If you don't know what "the rules" are for such interactions, ask several people for insights. You may be surprised at what you learn, and you may find that people, even the locals, perceive the rules in a variety of ways.

In addition, can you identify actions or behaviors that may be considered taboo? For example, do people greet only with their right hand but never with their left hand? As a culture sleuth, pay attention to the details of interactions around you, and try to identify if certain things are considered negative or offensive. In many parts of the world, for example, the left hand is associated with cleaning oneself when using the toilet. As a result, it is considered rude and offensive to use the left hand for other activities, such as giving an item to someone else or shaking hands. Cana, the student who wrote Profile 9 (Chapter 9), learned that this attitude is common in Ghana. She broke this unstated cultural rule twice within a few minutes but immediately recognized the strange looks she got from local Ghanaians and then used the opportunity to ask about what she had done. All of us will commit a cultural faux pas at some point, but the main point is to learn from those events and then try to match your behavior to the local expectations. Once you have identified a behavior that is considered taboo, it is a sign of respect to adjust how you act so that you avoid giving offense to the locals whenever possible.

Hierarchy and Power

Another area in which cultural values, assumptions, and expectations can be observed relates to relationships between people of different status. Individuals' attitudes regarding how their society functions need to be seen in action. In the United States, we don't have a king or hereditary nobility, although we do have celebrities who are often treated as elites. Perhaps because we lack a king, millions of U.S. Americans tuned in to watch Prince William marry Kate Middleton in 2011. We still have a love affair with the romantic notions of princes and princesses.

Moving beyond nobility, each culture has expectations regarding how power is used and how decisions are made. In the United States, the power difference between those of higher power and status and those of lower power and status is not very large. Although you likely call your professors "doctor" or "professor," it is common, if not encouraged, for students to interact with U.S. faculty on a fairly level playing field. Many faculty members, in the interest of encouraging critical thinking, invite their students to challenge them in class or argue alternate points of view. In many countries, these attitudes and approaches sound ludicrous because there is a greater power distance. In countries from China and Thailand to Chile and South Africa, university professors are treated as the authority on the subjects they teach. Students are expected to listen carefully to everything they say, absorb it, and regurgitate it for exams and papers. Students rarely challenge their professors in class, as one would be considered a snob to think one suddenly knew more than the professor. Needless to say, this attitude can be shocking to U.S. Americans who have been drilled on thinking for themselves and defending their own research and analysis.

In cultures across the globe, hierarchy is an everyday occurrence. One element of hierarchy is age. In many places, older people are treated with a great amount of respect, and a young person would be wise to treat a parent, grandparent, or older person with utmost dignity. This extends beyond the family sphere, where a grandfather or grandmother may give direction on almost every aspect of life, and touches on attitudes toward work and decision making. Age and seniority still play critical roles in business life across Asia, for example.

Another area of life in which hierarchy plays a role is between people of different status. In many cultures, it is common for secretaries, janitors, factory workers, and office workers to do only what they are told. In such cultures, managers and business owners are considered to be more knowledgeable about the needs of an office or business, so it would be considered offensive and presumptuous for a line worker to give suggestions to the boss. It is no surprise that in such cultures, titles and status are considered important. Even among the leading people in a company or organization, decisions are generally made by those of higher status or age.

Another example relates to interactions between people of high status and the janitors or servants who provide service to them. Students who study in India and other parts of South Asia, for example, are often shocked to find that locals interact very little with the "boys" who serve them. Many U.S. American students instinctively wish to talk with the men and boys who clean buildings, cook and serve meals, and run errands, whereas the local Indian elite speak to them fairly little, primarily to give orders. In India, there is a fairly strict and complex caste system, and the locals generally adhere to the traditional ways of interaction between people of different statuses. Although this, too, is changing gradually with each passing generation, it is still very different from the culture most U.S. Americans are familiar with.

In those parts of the world where multiple nationalities or ethnic groups have intermingled for centuries, it is common to find a hierarchy between ethnic or language groups, as well as competition between groups for political and economic influence. On the other side of the equation are cultures where hierarchy is smaller and where people are expected to express their opinions openly and directly. There may still be differences between people of different socioeconomic and educational background, but those differences are smaller than in cultures where hierarchy is more rigid.

How can you observe hierarchy and status while you are abroad, particularly if you are studying in a study center or with a faculty-led summer program? The first rule of thumb is to increase your interaction with the locals. You can't learn much about the attitudes and perspectives of the locals without meeting them and interacting with them. The second rule of thumb is to observe all of the people around you, even if you don't interact with them, to notice what they say and how they act toward each other. As a careful culture sleuth, you will begin to notice patterns of how people interact within your host environment, and over time you can make educated guesses about the reasons and expectations behind their actions. You will likely notice that many actions and behaviors are similar to yours, even if the reasons for those behaviors differ from your own.

Gender and Sexuality

Just like age, wealth, and other forms of social status, gender also affects how people think and act. Consider your own experiences growing up. If you are a guy, were you expected to work hard, compete in sports, or avoid crying and "be a man"? Were you treated differently than girls of your same age, including sisters? If you are a girl, what was your experience as a teenager? Do you expect boys to treat you as a "precious young lady," to open doors for you, and to be concerned for your well-being? Or have you always tried to compete with boys at sports or intellectual pursuits? How has your society shaped what is expected of young men and women, and do you like those expectations or fight against them?

Every culture sets expectations for how men and women, boys and girls treat each other. This goes far beyond fathering and bearing children, although biologically established gender does make a difference. It reaches into expectations of careers and earning power, how we spend time with people of our same gender and the opposite sex, and how we view certain behaviors, such as crying or yelling. In the United States, expectations regarding women and girls in the workforce have gradually been changing over the past century, and many women have broken "the glass ceiling" to attain CEO and other leadership positions in corporations, nonprofits, and government. But despite the gains for women in the workforce, not everything has changed, and it is well documented that women still earn less on average than men in similar positions. This suggests that societal expectations (this means cultural values) of what men and women do, including the rearing of children and families, have a direct influence on behavior and expectations.

One area in which social expectations can be seen is in attitudes toward marriage, divorce, and childbearing. Many decades ago in our country, people expected that nearly everyone, men and women, would get married at a fairly young age and would remain married "through thick and thin." Although premarital sex was common even back then, "shacking up" or living together before marriage was uncommon. Couples generally married when they had children, and divorce was rare and frowned upon. Since the Second World War, and particularly since the sexual revolution of the 1960s, attitudes toward marriage and divorce have changed substantially. It is now much more common for people to live together without getting married or to divorce when life gets difficult than it was two or three generations ago. A shift in attitudes toward same-sex relationships is also evident, and several states have now legalized same-sex marriage. All of this is evidence that cultural values do change, although slowly and often along generational lines. Many families and religious groups still encourage marriage and avoid divorce where possible, and there are still many who oppose same-sex marriage.

Another area where cultural values are shifting in our country is toward sex outside of marriage. It seems clear that sexual experimentation, both before marriage and within a marriage, has been common for centuries. What has changed are a variety of factors, including the openness of sex, the widespread practice of living together or cohabitating before marriage, and particularly the relatively new "hook-up" culture. Many U.S. students view sexual activity as common, easy, and expected, with "no strings attached." Although attitudes are similar in many countries around the world, it is not universal. In parts of Asia, Africa, and Latin America, casual sex is not common. Rather, sexual relations between two people are considered a sign of a special relationship much like marriage. In Nepal, for example, if a U.S. American guy has sex with a Nepalese girl, her family and friends will consider her married to the guy, regardless of his intentions. If he then leaves, her prospects of future marriage within her community are essentially gone, and she may be shunned for the rest of her life. Attitudes are somewhat different in parts of Africa, where if a man is found alone with a woman, he expects that her intention is to have sex with him. A study abroad student in western Africa found this out the hard way. She went to a party in a male student's dorm room with 8 or 10 other students. Later, when all the other guests had departed, the male student forced her to have sex with him, because he interpreted her willingness to be alone with him as a sign of her willingness to have sex. She was raped because she was unaware that her assumptions and his assumptions were very different. Study abroad students would do well to ask their program provider for information regarding local attitudes toward sex and sexuality and expectations for relationships between genders, so that they can interact knowledgeably with the locals and avoid putting themselves in situations where the rules and expectations are different than expected.

Another category of social expectations relates to machismo among guys. In many cultures, men's overt expressions of sexuality are tolerated if not encouraged. As a result of this culturally ingrained macho attitude, men often whistle at women as they walk down the street, invite them to their home or their bed, attempt to touch or pinch, or tell them how beautiful they are. This "cat calling" and "wolf whistling" can be shocking and disturbing to U.S. American women who are not used to such behavior. Some women enjoy the attention, at least at first, whereas others are shocked or offended. Study abroad advisors generally recommend that female students simply ignore the whistles, avoid looking at the men, and look forward as they walk confidently away from the situation. Ask your study abroad advisor or program provider about prevailing attitudes in the country where you will study or visit, so you can understand what behaviors to expect and how to deal with them. You can also learn some common phrases to use in situations where you may feel threatened or uncomfortable.

One final example of areas where expectations and behaviors differ from one culture to another relates to nudity. U.S. American students have generally grown up with expectations to cover their bodies in public. Even in high school locker rooms, the prevailing attitude is often to shower and dress in as much privacy as can be achieved. In many other cultures, people are much more comfortable with nudity in public or in groups. Finland, for example, has a wonderful tradition of bathing in a steam sauna. In almost every family, children go to the sauna nude several times per week with all members of their family, male and female. In the summertime, families spend time in the countryside, where saunas are ubiquitous and where families join together to visit the sauna. As a result, most Finns are comfortable being naked in such groups, and they are shocked to find that U.S. American men and women are uncomfortable in such situations. Showering or bathing in public or semipublic settings is common in other cultures, from the Russian banya and Turkish baths to group baths in Japan and showers in parts of Africa.

I am not suggesting that you suddenly lose all of your inhibitions or put yourself in mixed-gender situations where you do not feel comfortable. I am suggesting that you put on your culture sleuth hat, ask questions, and find out about local patterns and traditions. Study abroad students can arrange to participate in a local tradition such as a Finnish sauna, Russian banya, or Turkish bath with people of the same gender. You may not feel completely comfortable about it the first time, but you may actually enjoy the experience and have a better sense of why these group bathing experiences have developed and remained strong for centuries. You may also find yourself becoming more comfortable in your own skin as you see life from a different perspective.

Cleanliness

Another element of relationships can be seen in attitudes toward cleanliness. Study abroad students are routinely shocked when they travel to another country, even in western Europe, and find that others have different attitudes toward both personal hygiene and cleanliness in the home, office, or community. Let's begin with the personal side of this topic. In the United States, it is common for people to shower or bathe on a daily basis. Many college students have the habit of taking hot showers that might last 10 to 30 minutes, and a few take multiple showers each day. They may enjoy luxuriating in the heat and steam of a shower or bath. In addition, they may feel that daily showers, plus daily shaving, are essential for keeping clean and staying healthy.

In many countries, including in western Europe, daily showers or baths are not expected as part of one's daily routine. In fact, taking long daily showers is considered excessive for many people, particularly in places where water is limited. In some regions, the green movement emphasizes the environmental impact of such practices and the added cost of high water use. In other regions, clean water may not be available 24/7. U.S. American study abroad students may be shocked to learn that some Europeans shower two or three times per week and that their showers often last just four or five minutes at most. These individuals likely believe that this amount of showering is sufficient for keeping clean and recognize that short showers are better for the environment. In parts of Africa, Asia, and Latin America, people may wash themselves in a river or lake, pour water over the heads from a bucket, or take a sponge bath just once or twice per week. Local attitudes and expectations around showering, bathing, and personal hygiene thus vary widely.

As a culture sleuth, pay attention to how often people shower or take baths, as well as to what people say about using shower facilities, particularly in home stays. Realize that people in other countries probably have different expectations regarding personal hygiene and cleanliness. It is not that their attitudes are wrong or right but that they are just different from yours. If you live in a dormitory or apartment with locals, ask them about what they do or what they expect in terms of personal hygiene, then make educated guesses regarding the values, resources, and historical trends that have shaped those expectations.

Another area in which attitudes toward cleanliness are visible is in the home. Study abroad students routinely observe practices and habits that differ from their own. In places like Japan and Russia, people take off their shoes or boots when entering a home, then put on a pair of slippers or other footwear for use in the rest of the house. This habit has the benefit of keeping dirt or mud in only one part of the home rather than allowing it to spread throughout the building. People in Japan also tend to change to a different pair of slippers when they need to use the toilet in order to avoid spreading contamination to other rooms. Japanese people who hold these expectations are often shocked by the cavalier behavior of American visitors who ignore such traditions. Similar examples can be found around the globe.

Where possible, ask questions of your study abroad advisor and program staff to learn more about common practices in the home and community. In addition, pay attention to the actions and attitudes of the people you meet. You will likely learn more about their society, history, and values than you expect. You will gain a greater appreciation of the people you meet and understand their behaviors and expectations much better than before. These habits and skills are essential parts of intercultural learning and understanding.

6

LESS VISIBLE ELEMENTS
OF CULTURE
Communication Styles, Religion, and Time

Profile 6: Grier King

By the time my study abroad experience ended, I found myself to be different in many ways. It was an unforgettable experience, and an experience that is sometimes difficult to put into words. It helped me to grow in a way that Wake Forest could not. I went through obvious changes like learning a new language and learning how to become more independent, but my time in Madrid also helped me to become more open-minded and to discover the vast differences in culture and societies that encompass the world in which we live.

One of the biggest changes that occurred within me was the altering of my perception of the world. I had never traveled much before I went abroad, only to a couple countries in the Caribbean, but the areas that I visited were so full of tourists that I didn't notice the local culture, and I had spent only a maximum of a week in these places. Living in a host family for three and a half months and becoming fully immersed in a completely different culture made me realize that America is not the only country on the planet. Living in America, I often feel so removed from the rest of the world and tend to focus only on our culture, but once I was able to experience other countries and their people firsthand, I was able to see the diversity that makes up the planet. I became more open-minded when living in Spain and visiting other countries, because I saw that each country is different, and there are different ideas and beliefs valued in each. I had always heard of these concepts in textbooks, but being able to encounter them helped me to be more open and understanding. By seeing these drastic differences among other countries, it helped me to be more open to people in America who are different from myself; for example, if I were walking down a street and someone bumps into me without saying "excuse me," I'm not completely offended by it anymore. That individual could come from a background where you don't say "excuse me" or give a friendly smile to a stranger.

Studying in Spain has made me want more intercultural competence. I am so happy to be learning another language, and I wish I could speak more. I want to be able to relate to people across the world, not limiting myself to people of my own race and background. I want to definitely continue learning and practicing Spanish. It is something that is useful in life and will allow me to become more involved in the Hispanic culture. I am majoring in psychology and hope to become a social worker, which will most likely involve me working with people from other cultures and backgrounds. Luckily, after my study abroad experience, my thinking and beliefs will not be limited, and I will be able to communicate with these people in a more positive manner.

I did resist some changes. In Spanish culture, people tend to move slower, but I don't want to lose my ambition and zeal for life. I had a hard time "slowing down," and I don't think I want to slow down. At times, it is important, but I hope my "American ambition" will stay with me through life. I also didn't want to lose a sense of who I am or my background when in Spain. I was there for so long that I found myself fully adapting to the local environment and culture, but I never wanted to change my background or where I came from. No matter what your culture is like, it is an important aspect that makes you who you are, and it should be something that is celebrated and valued. We identify with a culture, and it helps us to identify who we are as individuals and helps to facilitate other interactions among people.

In Chapter 5 we discussed how relationships are shaped by cultural values and expectations, how individuals function within the context of their family and group, how gender and sexuality are influenced by widely held cultural expectations, and how attitudes regarding cleanliness reveal cultural norms. This chapter explores a few other elements of cultural patterns and values that are generally noticeable only as you observe and interact with your hosts. These are additional elements of culture and relationships that are "below the waterline" in the metaphor of culture as an iceberg. The good news is that patterns and norms reveal themselves when we pay attention to how people speak and act.

Communication Styles

Let us begin this chapter with the fairly broad topic of communication. This encompasses a large number of elements, from how people communicate with spoken language to body language and other forms of nonverbal communication, including what they do with their hands and feet. It is through communication patterns that core elements of culture are revealed, hence the need to watch and communicate with others to identify cultural expectations and values.

Have you ever stopped to think about your preferred methods of communication? Are you generally shy when initiating a conversation, making a phone call, or asking for directions or assistance? Or are you a talkative person who strikes up conversations with ease? Do you like to communicate your feelings and desires directly with those around you, or do you prefer to keep your feelings, fears, or frustrations hidden most of the time? Regardless of your personal preferences and skills in communicating, the ways you communicate with language reveal much about your own cultural background and expectations.

Researchers who study cross-cultural communication often describe two main trends around the world: direct forms of communication and indirect forms. Most people who grow up in the United States follow the patterns of direct communication. This means that we generally say what we think, ask direct questions, expect direct answers, and want to get quickly to the point of a conversation. In addition, we are comfortable telling others "no" or turning down requests for assistance. We are taught to speak clearly and answer the question. We do not need to know the people we are speaking with to understand their questions or responses, and we often do not need to understand their status or where we fit in the proverbial pecking order. Cultures that favor direct communication also generally require less information about the context in which that communication is taking place. Hence, *direct forms of communication* often go hand in hand with what is called *low context*.

In contrast, in many parts of the world, people use more indirect forms of communication. Their conversations are generally shaped more by the context in which people communicate, including the status and gender of those involved. This *indirect communication style* is therefore *high context*, because meaning and answers are communicated as much by what is not said as by what is said. It is common among indirect, high-context conversations for people to infer meaning from the other person's status, body language, choice of words, and other verbal clues. When people want to say no in such conversations, they find indirect ways to express a negative rather than say it outright. This implies, however, that high-context communicators know much more about each other, the topic they are discussing, and what is expected of both parties than do people in low-context cultures. Many Asian and Middle Eastern cultures favor indirect, high-context modes of communication, whereas many European cultures favor direct, low-context forms of interaction. All cultures use a mixture of direct, low-context communication in certain situations and indirect, high-context expressions in other situations. For example, you have probably found yourself in situations where you wanted to say or express a negative but didn't want to say it directly, so you tried to imply your meaning with other aspects of communication, such as body language, irony, or a popular expression.

So what is this thing we are calling *context*? It is a combination of many different things. It goes beyond observing the age and gender of both parties in the conversation. It requires both parties to notice each other's status. It includes a sense of connectedness, both to each other and to others in society. High-context cultures generally emphasize the need to maintain social harmony and peace, so conversations are moderated intentionally to minimize conflict. In addition, many languages have more than one way to say the word *you*. Those who have learned Spanish or French or Russian have encountered this challenge of knowing the difference between *tu* and *usted*, *tu* and *vous*, ты and вы. Native speakers of the language instinctively use one form or the other in various situations based on their perception of the person they are addressing and the context for the communication. In addition, many languages also have multiple words considered "honorifics," such as *your highness, your honor, sir, ma'am*, and so on. People are expected to know which words of honor are appropriate for each situation, as it would be inappropriate to use the same honor words with your neighbor as you would for the company president or the king, for example. When people in high-context cultures meet someone they have not known before, they may spend minutes or hours getting to know the person, asking questions about his or her family and background, in order to determine how their communication should proceed and how they are connected. In contrast, people in low-context cultures do not feel the need to understand their communication partner thoroughly, so they often dive right into a conversation with only a few pleasantries.

To illustrate this, let's use the fictitious example of an interaction between a direct, low-context U.S. American student and an indirect, high-context Japanese student who are enrolled in a course together and are assigned to work on a joint project. Let's say the professor has assigned them to meet as a group, research a topic, and then report to the class in three weeks. At their first meeting together, it is no surprise that these two students approach this assignment quite differently, particularly if they have not spent much time together previously. The U.S. American student expects that they will get right to work, discuss possible topics, debate openly the various angles, and then come up with a game plan for getting the assignment done. The U.S. American does not feel a strong need to know the Japanese student very well in order to complete the assignment. The Japanese student, on the other hand, expects to get to know his or her counterpart and to share insights first in order to determine which of them is best suited for different parts of the assignment. The Japanese student likely feels a strong need to find common ground and agreement, to understand each other's perspective, whereas the U.S. American student might be comfortable with expressing disagreement or different approaches to the assignment.

At their first meeting, the two students need to arrange for future meetings. The U.S. American student might ask directly about possible days and times that would work for the next meeting, expecting the Japanese student to say directly whether certain times work or do not work. The Japanese student, in contrast, may find it hard to say no to proposed times, feeling that the U.S. American student should be able to read body language or derive meaning from responses that do not express full agreement. Phrases such as "Okay, let me think about that time" or "That is very interesting" may be attempts to say no to proposed times. The Japanese student, coming from a high-context cultural perspective, might even say yes to times that don't work, expecting that the context in which the conversation takes place will reveal the meaning "no." People who naturally use high-context, indirect forms of communication often feel a strong need to "save face" in many situations, as we will discuss in the next section.

One might ask why certain cultures favor high-context, indirect forms of communication. Edward T. Hall believes that high-context systems evolved over time. Historically, in countries like Japan, there were distinct social classes and a rigid hierarchy, so reading other people's body language and understanding social expectations for one's group were essential for survival. Hall also noted that there is a continuum of context and directness rather than extremes. Some cultures favor a combination of directness and indirectness, whereas others lean more to one side or the other (Hall, 1976/1981).

What role does body language play in how we communicate? Some researchers claim that 80% or more of what we communicate comes not through the words we use but through how we say them, including the tone of voice we use and what we do with our face, body, and hands. Each of us has likely used humor or irony to say one thing but imply something else. "Reading" another person's voice and body language is essential for understanding their intent and meaning. It should therefore come as no surprise that body language in other cultures can mean different things in your culture. Let's take the "thumbs up" signal, which was commonly used in the United States after World War II and was regularly portrayed in the 1970s television show *Happy Days*. Many U.S. Americans indicate their pleasure or agreement with something by closing their fist while raising their thumb. The opposite meaning is given with the thumb down. Do you think that pointing your thumbs up carries the same meaning in places where they have never watched *Happy Days*? Is it possible that lifting your thumb in other cultures might have a negative or derogatory meaning, rather than a positive one? The "OK" sign is an example of a hand expression that carries different meanings in other parts of the world. To some the

OK sign indicates approval, whereas others, such as those in Russia and Turkey, consider it an obscene gesture. As a culture sleuth, pay attention to the hand signals people use, and do your best to understand the meaning that is intended when they are used. Keep in mind that hand signals considered neutral or positive here in the United States might be considered rude or obscene in other places.

Other aspects of body language include facial expressions used during communication or when listening to someone else. When you are happy and engaged with your best friends, talking about the latest gossip or sports event, you can easily tell if others are happy and in agreement. In such conversations, significant information and meaning are derived through your body language. The same is likely true for the opposite extreme, when we feel the need to communicate dissent or dissatisfaction with something. Many teenagers learn the art of rolling their eyes, showing disappointment or resistance, or completely shutting down. Similar things are done in other cultures, although the common facial expressions may vary from those used in the United States.

Another example of body language relates to what we do with our feet when sitting. Have you ever thought about what you are doing with your feet when sitting with a group of people? I never did when I grew up. However, in some cultures it is considered offensive to show the bottoms of your feet to someone across from you. For this reason, in those cultures, people who cross their legs while sitting are expected to point the soles of the feet downward rather than outward. In yet other cultures, it is considered rude to put your feet on a chair or table nearby, as one student found out.

Madeline Skahill

After attending Oktoberfest, my two friends and I hopped the train that would take us to the Munich airport. After sitting on the train for 20 minutes and having one of the most exhausting weekends of my life, I decided to put my feet up on the empty chair that was facing me. Within seconds, I was scolded by a cranky old German woman. Obviously knowing not one word of German, I grew extremely confused why this old woman was yelling at me. I immediately sat up to try to understand, and after minutes of her pointing out the seat across from me and then pointing at my shoe, I realized that it was completely unacceptable to put your feet up on a train. Within minutes the entire car was staring at me, while of course my two friends were hysterically laughing. We could understand they were talking badly about young Americans, and one of my friends could understand that the German people kept saying the word "typical." I had never felt as completely singled out as an American girl as I did at that moment, and I could not wait to get off that train.

One other aspect of body language involves how far apart people stand and whether they touch each other when speaking. In the United States, it is common for people to stand 18 to 24 inches apart for most conversations. We have a relatively high amount of *personal space* that we like to have around us. If someone invades our personal space, we generally move backward or sideward in order to regain the amount of space we have come to expect. In contrast, in some other parts of the world, such as Turkey, Spain, and parts of the Middle East, the expected personal space is much smaller, perhaps just 10 or 12 inches. People show respect and closeness for others by standing closer together, holding hands, or touching the other person on the shoulder or arm. In many countries, women and girls often hold hands while walking on the street as a sign of friendship. U.S. American study abroad students can be shocked at first when observing situations where the rules for interaction are different from what they have learned.

Regardless of the situation, culture sleuths aim to observe how people in another country or culture interact, what hand and facial expressions they use, what body movements and hand signals are common, and how close they stand. When puzzled or confused about why people in the host culture do something specific, they ask questions of the locals, seeking understanding and perspective. Then, where appropriate, they adapt their body language and communication style to fit into each new situation, and this includes avoiding actions or gestures that are considered rude or obscene. Learning and following the expectations and norms in the host culture is a sign of respect for your hosts.

Respect, Shame, and Saving Face

In many cultures, the concepts of respect, shame, and "face" play an essential role in how people communicate and act. One's "face" is his or her reputation and standing in the community. When there is disagreement or conflict, people often seek ways to "save" their own reputation or that of others by finding a compromise or solution that is satisfactory to both parties. Doing so helps them preserve respect while avoiding shame. You have likely needed to save face in a variety of situations, particularly those involving conflict. It is natural that you wish to receive respect from others, avoid feeling shame for your actions, and interact comfortably with others.

In many cultures, people are often more keenly aware of face, respect, and reputation, particularly in high-context cultures where the hierarchy is stronger and their social status plays a key role in how they act. In fact, the concept of "saving face" applies to the individual and to others in the family or group. In group-oriented cultures, one person's poor actions may cause shame or disrespect for the entire group. Members of a family or ethnic community may experience intense shame for the misdeeds of one individual, and for this reason people in the group try hard to avoid behaviors that are not fully endorsed by the group.

Study abroad students studying in Asia, to choose just one example, may notice a variety of ways in which saving face is manifested by their hosts. If a U.S. American student invites an Asian student to an event or party, for example, but the time selected conflicts with the Asian student's schedule, the Asian student will tend to find a polite, indirect way to communicate "no" (but not say "no") in order to avoid the conflict inherent in saying "no" and to maintain harmony within the group. In some cases, the Asian student may rearrange her entire schedule rather than turn down the U.S. American student's invitation. In other cases, the Asian student may simply describe other things going on that day or time, expecting the U.S. American will "read between the lines" and understand what is meant. The Asian may feel the need to protect her own face as well as that of the American through using an indirect method of communication.

Although we often think of saving face in regard to Asian and Middle Eastern cultures, the concept of safeguarding one's reputation and status and avoiding shame is common throughout the world. As you interact with your hosts, pay attention to how they resolve issues of conflict and maintain harmony. Doing so will help you identify cultural patterns and values relating to harmony, agreement, and respect for others.

Religion and Faith Traditions

Many of the cultural values, traditions, and expectations we have discussed so far have been shaped by the teachings and traditions of churches, religions, and faith communities. Christianity, Judaism, Islam, Buddhism, Shintoism, Sikhism, and other faith traditions have directly shaped the expectations and norms of local cultures in a variety of ways. Even within Christianity, there are numerous different traditions, ranging from Catholicism, Lutheranism, and the Anglican traditions in western Europe to Eastern Orthodoxy in eastern and southern Europe, Africa, and the Caucasus, as well as Christian traditions throughout Asia (particularly South Korea), Africa, and Latin America. And there are numerous traditions within Judaism, Islam, and Buddhism as well.

Study abroad students generally will not understand all the varieties of faith traditions in their study abroad country or the places they visit. But you can begin learning about the main religious traditions before going abroad and continue to learn while in-country. First, identify the two or three largest churches or faith communities in your study abroad country. Then, find a book or Internet resource that describes the main principles of belief and patterns of worship in each one. You may not fully understand all of the teachings or all of the reasons why individuals worship the way they do, but at least you can identify key points that can help you find more information when you arrive at your study abroad program. Pay attention to what the church or faith tradition teaches regarding expected behavior. More important, look for the core values that are at the heart of this religion. These may include respect for life, respect for deity, attention to one's ancestors, charity for others, and so on.

All churches and faith traditions establish patterns regarding how people should interact with one another. These guidelines or principles, taught over hundreds of years, create a significant number of expectations that most people internalize, as well as the words and phrases that communicate those expectations. Keep in mind that the ways such teachings and expectations are communicated or interpreted often vary from one part of the world to another. If you have an opportunity to attend a church service or visit a temple, mosque, or synagogue, take advantage of the chance to observe how the locals practice their religious traditions.

As a culture sleuth, pay attention to how men, women, and children act and interact in their churches or buildings. Do they bow or cross themselves in a certain way? Do men and women worship separately or together? What can you interpret based on how the locals interact with each other and how they respond to you? How do they dress? In many faith traditions, women are expected to cover their head with a scarf and to wear a skirt or a dress, not jeans or shorts, and men are expected to wear long slacks rather than shorts. Avoid cultural faux pas, such as sitting on religious objects. Several years ago a U.S. American tourist had the terrible idea of having a photo taken when sitting atop a statue of Buddha. According to news reports, that individual was nearly arrested for breaking local laws regarding respect for religious shrines and objects. Be respectful when visiting a church, synagogue, shrine, or temple by walking slowly, being completely quiet or talking with a very low voice, and showing reverence for local traditions. Laughing and joking when visiting another religion's holy site is considered disrespectful. You may be expected to dress differently, such as putting on a head covering or scarf and wearing slacks or a skirt rather than shorts. Ask your advisor or program leader for more information about such things.

Churches and faith traditions also have beliefs about deity and about what happens after death. Some faith traditions, including Christianity, teach that humans have a spirit or soul that continues to live, with hope of heaven or an afterlife. Other traditions regard death as the end of one's existence.

When learning about the teachings and beliefs of other churches and faith traditions, look for the features that give meaning to the believers and adherents of those traditions. You may be pleasantly surprised at how much your personal beliefs may have in common with the teachings of these churches or religions.

Approaches to Time and Schedules

One other feature of communication relates to attitudes toward time. Researchers who study cultures around the world have identified two main trends regarding how we use our time. These are called *short-term* and *long-term orientations,* or *monochronic* and *polychronic* approaches to time, respectively. Many people in the United States have a short-term (monochronic) orientation to time. Common elements of a short-term orientation include an emphasis on being on time for appointments or meetings, using time efficiently, and expecting that others are sensitive to your time and needs. People with a short-term orientation treat time as a limited commodity that should be used wisely. "Time is money" is a common mantra. As a result, there tends to be more emphasis on keeping to schedules, getting through an agenda, and getting things accomplished within a specific time frame.

In contrast is a long-term orientation, which says that time is unlimited. People with a long-term (polychronic) orientation toward time, such as many in the Middle East and Latin America, do not feel as compelled to worry about keeping schedules, getting a set of tasks done within a specific time frame, or covering all items on an agenda. The long-term orientation also emphasizes the importance of maintaining harmony, focusing on relationships, and prioritizing the needs of others over agendas. As a result, people with a long-term orientation are not worried when meetings do not start on time or when others show up for events later than the scheduled time because they trust that any meeting or discussion that is essential will take place eventually. Many describe this kind of orientation as "Latin time." Individuals who are not accustomed to long-term orientations to time are often bothered or offended by others who have different habits regarding time and schedules.

The important thing for study abroad students to realize is that fundamental cultural patterns and expectations relating to time affect many other things in a culture. Students who are time oriented and task oriented often struggle at first to understand "how people can live like this." Many U.S. students studying in Australia, for example, are often struck by the low-key, low-stress attitudes of the local students, who tend to see relationships and enjoying life as higher priorities than homework and class attendance (see Profile 8 in the next chapter). Many U.S. students studying in parts of Africa and Latin America tend to get frustrated when meetings do not start on time or when people arrive for a 7:00 p.m. event at 8:00 p.m. or even 9:00 p.m.

As a culture sleuth, pay attention to how people act, as well as how they talk about time, meetings, and schedules. Where appropriate, ask questions of the locals about how they approach time, so you can look "below the waterline" and identify broad patterns for behavior and expectations in the local culture. This will help you understand the local perspective and enjoy the time you spend in-country. Keep in mind that many people use a combination of long-term and short-term orientation strategies in their lives, depending on their circumstances.

Uncertainty and Ambiguity

Another common element of culture relates to how comfortable people are with uncertainty in their lives. Some cultures try to avoid uncertainty by making things clear and explicit, whereas in other cultures people are comfortable with uncertainty and ambiguity. As you might guess, direct, low-context cultures tend to avoid uncertainty, whereas indirect, high-context cultures tend to be comfortable with uncertainty and ambiguity to a larger degree.

Consider yourself and how you were raised. Did your parents or teachers tend to identify every assignment or expectation they had? Or did they give you general instructions or examples when giving you an assignment? Do you find yourself wishing that all of your professors would make their expectations clear and complete? Or are you comfortable with things being a little unclear, as this creates an opportunity for you to shine?

A student from a direct, low-context culture who is accustomed to receiving clear instructions and knowing exactly what is expected of her can feel a little out of place in a culture where instructions are general or ambiguous. She might feel frustrated by situations in which the locals seem to know what to do but without talking about how precisely to do it or what steps need to be taken. The keys for the culture sleuth are to pay attention to what others say and do and to ask questions when necessary. Of course, it is also essential to be patient with yourself and others as you observe the actions of others and try to make an educated guess about what you are expected to do or say.

As you learn about your host culture and watch how others behave, you may find yourself forming judgments about them. It will take time to notice patterns of behavior in how people communicate, what role respect and saving face place in their interactions, and how they approach time. Sometimes you might be completely surprised by how others respond to something you do, as Cana discovered during a meal (see Profile 9 in Chapter 9) or as Madeline found while riding the train (see the Student Story in this chapter). The logical next step is for you to make educated guesses about why people have acted the way they did, ask questions about their actions or expectations, and then learn from the experience. If you feel comfortable with it, you can also adapt your own behavior to match the local pattern, as this will allow you to test the theories you have made regarding cultural expectations. You will have the opportunity to learn more about your hosts and yourself and see culture in action. These are important intercultural skills to learn and develop.

7

YOUR IDENTITY

Profile 7: Abigail

Through my study abroad experience, I feel I have grown exponentially in a few specific areas in my everyday life. Before my abroad experience, I feel that I was going through the motions of life; I would spend endless hours studying each week, hang out with the same people, have the same daily routines, and look at the same scenes around campus and at home. I had gotten completely comfortable about everything in my everyday life. I was comfortable with continuing the same relationships, continuing similar classes, and continuing at the same school and social scene for the past two years. Needless to say, I was taking for granted a lot of the things in my life because of the ease I felt around them. This old way of life was haggard and needed a change. This was why I chose to go abroad in the fall of 2011. I felt that this would give me the boost I needed to be able to get through the next two wonderful years in college and really enjoy them.

Through going abroad, I got the ruffle of feathers that I needed to get back on my feet and stop just going through the motions of life. Through my abroad experience, I have become more independent, more able to adapt in tough situations, and more accepting of people that are different from me. I feel that in these changes, I have become more mature and culturally aware, and therefore I have made useful skills that I will use for the rest of my life. I feel that I have embraced all of these changes because I have used them in my everyday life since returning from abroad. I feel that because when I was abroad, I had to live on my own and cook, clean, and take care of myself; I learned independence. Now that I am back at Wake Forest, I have moved off campus into an apartment, so all of my independence skills learned abroad have been directly applicable to my life at school. I again have to clean and cook and live on my own, so being independent is a necessity here. I feel that I have had to adapt in different situations here through my job search, so that is a big feat for me.

These are some qualities I have developed and embraced since returning from abroad.

My goals and values have changed in a few ways since being abroad. I feel that my goals in life after being abroad are less about my future in jobs and money and more about being happy and accomplishing social and emotional battles. I have moved away from the notion that work is the most important part of my life and have realized that more important things like happiness and relationships should be a first priority. This has affected my values and morals as a whole to become more based off of emotions rather than material items and employment. While things like sustaining a good life and having a good, well-respected job are still very important to me and the success of my life, I have made room for other things in my values and morals that have reshaped the way that I am.

Overall my study abroad experience was the most amazing experience that I have had thus far, and I hope that I will be able to continue to use the intercultural skills I gained abroad for the remainder of my life.

One of the amazing aspects of studying and traveling abroad is that we learn new things about ourselves in the process of learning about others. Many students returning from study abroad report that they have developed new skills and fresh perspectives about the world and the diversity of the human experience. Others find hidden strengths, interests, or abilities they had not expected. Some, including me, come home from abroad and change their major or pursue a different field of study because of new insights about themselves or their interests in life. At the same time, going abroad can also challenge students' identities, putting stress on things they thought they knew about themselves or altering previously held beliefs. The culture shock caused by those stresses requires us to adjust in various ways (see Chapter 8).

As you prepare to study abroad, it is useful to take a few moments for self-reflection. What are your goals for your abroad experience, and are they connected with your identity in some way? Did you select your program or host country because of a family heritage in that location? Perhaps your grandparents or distant relatives lived there, and you have always wanted to return to or visit that country or location. Is being an Italian American or Korean American a key part of who you are? Or have you selected a study abroad country not because of any family connection but because it fascinates you? Do you have artistic, engineering, scientific, or business skills that have led you to that program or location? Whatever your reasons for picking a program or host country, it is useful to reflect on how you see yourself, as well as how others might perceive you.

In previous chapters we discussed ways in which cultural norms, values, assumptions, and expectations influence how large groups of people act and think. But cultural values don't determine every single aspect of how individuals behave. This chapter explores identities, personality and personal preferences, and learning styles, which manifest themselves at the individual level rather than at the group or national level.

Each person throughout the world is unique, including you. This is true about members of your family, your neighborhood, your high school, your church or synagogue, and much more. So although it is valuable for culture sleuths to look for national or regional trends, they should also keep in mind that many behaviors are shaped by individual choices and preferences. After all, when you go abroad you will be interacting with individuals, not faceless masses.

Who You Are

Take a few minutes to think about what makes you unique. What makes you, you? How would you describe yourself to people who know you well? How would you describe yourself to someone you have just met, who doesn't know anything about you? Would you start off with your physical features, such as the color of your hair, your height, or your weight? Would you tell about your family or friends? Would you emphasize your skills or experience playing a sport, participating in art or music, or pursuing a specific major or academic interest such as debate or writers' club? Or would you tell more personal things, such as what church or faith community you participate in, what schools you have attended, where you grew up, the kinds of books or newspapers you like to read, the games you like to play, the projects you have designed or built, or your other interests?

As you can imagine, you would probably say different things to different people, depending on the circumstances of such a conversation and who else is involved. There are dozens of interests, skills, and personal details that make each of us unique. Each of us has multiple traits and interests, and we emphasize them, or use unique combinations of them, in a variety of different ways depending on the circumstances and whom we are with. These traits and interests shape a variety of identities that we carry inside of us each day.

Take a few minutes to write down the 10 or 20 words or phrases that best describe you, and keep this list to review when you return home from abroad. Some of these may be visible to the naked eye, but most of them will not be. If you were to rank order these words or phrases beginning with the most important, which of them do you think describes the essential you? How would other people get to see or know these things about you, and what makes you unique? How many of these 10 or 20 descriptors would be visible from your physical appearance? How many of them would require someone to get to know you more deeply before that person became aware of your identity or personality?

When we meet new people in the United States, we tend to ask questions about where they live, where they are from, where they work or go to school, or whether they follow a certain team or sport. In other parts of the world, people might first ask about people's family, what school and church or synagogue they attend, or what newspaper they read. In both cases, humans try to place a new person into a known context, establish rapport, and find common ground. Our cultural values and our identities, personality, and personal interests shape how we answer such questions about ourselves and what questions we ask about others. Of course, we also try to place people into a known context by looking at their appearance, including the color and style of their clothing, shoes, and accessories.

As you travel abroad, keep your ears open for the kinds of questions people in your host culture ask when they first meet you or someone else who is new to them. What do the questions they ask reveal about their own identities or what is important to them? Can you identify patterns of questions that are commonly asked or what is not asked when people meet each other for the first time?

It should be self-evident that your identities are not wrong or right; they are just you. It is common for us to describe ourselves in different ways in different contexts. You may find that certain areas of your life that you have taken for granted are suddenly challenged a bit while you are abroad, whereas other identities provide more strength or more context for the situations in which you live. You may also find opportunities to explore things that you would like to add to yourself. For example, many study abroad students identify one of their goals for going abroad as developing a world-mindedness or global perspective. Especially for those who have never traveled abroad, the ability to see other parts of the world, meet other people, and see things from their point of view becomes an eye-opening experience that helps them create a new identity for themselves. They often come home more engaged with global issues and eager to travel abroad more often in the future, including to work. Heather, who wrote Profile 3 (see Chapter 3), is only one of many students who have expressed an interest in an international career after graduation.

Study abroad students often find that their experience abroad places their identities and cultural values under stress, challenging them to think more deeply about who they are and what they value in life. Often it is hard to separate our cultural values and expectations from our personal preferences and identities. For example, many U.S. American students who study in Europe have been asked pointed, challenging questions about U.S. foreign policy, about our presidents and their actions around the world, and about our country's role in past events, such as the Cold War, wars in Iraq and Afghanistan, or the "Arab Spring." Some students find themselves agreeing with criticisms of the activities of the United States abroad, whereas others tend to defend our country or leaders or explain different issues or episodes. In the process, our identity as a U.S. citizen is challenged, and we respond according to the situation. Such experiences can also strengthen certain attitudes or lead us to adjust our opinions, depending on the circumstances.

Personality and Personal Preferences

Another aspect of our identities that makes us each unique is our personality. This goes beyond simply being outgoing, fun, patient, shy, diligent, or energetic and touches on many things that make us unique. Some of this includes the types of things you like to do, as well as personal preferences, such as your favorite colors, what types of vehicles you prefer to drive, or what music you like.

Personalities can be shaped by aspects of culture, but they often are extremely varied and can run counter to things in a culture. For example, it is common to find introverts and extroverts in every culture. People in Finland, for example, are generally quiet and reserved in public and in many private situations, yet there are bubbly people who are outgoing even in public who run counter to that pattern.

Your personal preferences will shape many aspects of your experience abroad. For example, many students prefer not to eat seafood, pork, or certain kinds of vegetables, yet they study in a country where those items are consumed on a regular basis. When you are faced with opportunities to try new foods, do you dig in and relish the chance to try something, or do you shy away? There is no wrong or right answer, because each person and each situation is unique. Although I personally encourage my students and my children to be open to new experiences ("You never know whether you will like it unless you try it"), I also know that I avoid certain things if I can. One should not violate his or her moral code or religious beliefs simply to try a new dish or beverage. Of course, from a health and safety perspective, it is best not to eat foods that are prepared in sketchy conditions or that have been standing out, perhaps in the hot sun, for hours on end.

Personal preferences are also visible in the clothing you wear, how you style your hair, and your overall appearance. Some students prefer to assert their individuality through their hair color, makeup, jewelry, piercings, or tattoos. Others assert their personality through clothing, shoes, shopping, or sports.

Jim Kavalec

After spending a semester in Milan, Italy, I have noticed several changes in how I view myself and how I view the world around me. My sense of culture, personal values, and interests were all affected by my time abroad. One of the first things I noticed when I first arrived in Italy was how midwestern I truly am. Although I had always described myself as a Midwest boy to my friends at Wake Forest, this always felt more like a label to me than an actual identity. Once I was in a foreign country, though, I realized that I truly represented midwestern culture. My flannel shirts, baseball hats, boots, and affinity for country music contrasted much more sharply with the Italian culture than other American subcultures. While in Italy, I absolutely refused to give up this part of me and continued to wear the clothes that made me happy, even though they clearly made me look American. Before going to Italy, I never realized how much I valued these parts of myself, but now I appreciate them much more.

In this example, Jim relates how being in Italy sharpened his attachment to his personal style and preferences. Being abroad helped him to appreciate the things he grew up with and to feel comfortable being different from the local population. In other cases, study abroad students find themselves adopting local styles or exploring a new look. The main thing to keep in mind is that you are a unique individual with a unique combination of interests, skills, and preferences. Likewise, the local population comprises a diverse range of individuals who may have very different attitudes about many issues, even though they seem similar on the outside. Culture sleuths look for patterns of both similarity and difference when interacting with the locals.

One location where personalities and personal preferences come into clear view is in our housing. While abroad, you might live in an apartment or dorm with other U.S. American students, with host nationals, or perhaps with a mixture of U.S. American and international students. Many students live in a home stay arrangement, where they live with a local family and perhaps another study abroad student. In all of these locations, you will need to navigate the personalities and preferences, as well as the cultural expectations, of those with whom you live. Your housing will give you numerous opportunities to practice the important intercultural skills of being flexible, adapting to new environments, resolving conflict, and communicating with people from diverse backgrounds. Danny, the student who wrote Profile 13 (Chapter 9), found that his home stay situation offered both opportunities and challenges that helped him develop new insights about himself.

Learning Styles

Another aspect that affects each of us involves our learning styles. Have you ever stopped to think about the ways you learn best? Have you noticed that you enjoy certain types of classes (such as art or hands-on subjects) but dislike other forms of learning (such as lecture classes)? Do you prefer reading and theoretical learning, or do you try to avoid reading when possible? Have you ever taken a learning styles inventory or talked with a career advisor regarding the ways you learn best?

David Kolb, a scholar who developed experiential learning theory, identified four main styles of learning (Kolb, 1984; Kolb & Kolb, 2005). These four styles are also the key parts of the learning cycle. Students use these modes of learning as they have new experiences and then make meaning from those experiences (Zull, 2012). These modes of learning are as follows:

- *Concrete experience:* doing something or having an experience
- *Reflective observation:* reflecting on that experience or event
- *Abstract conceptualization:* forming a conclusion based on that experience
- *Active experimentation:* planning an experiment to test out what we have learned

According to Kolb, the first and third stages are on opposite sides of a continuum between doing and abstractly conceptualizing, whereas the second and fourth stages are on opposite sides of a continuum between quiet reflection and active experimentation. Most people prefer one area along each continuum, depending on the situation in which they find themselves. Here again, each person is unique and has different strengths and interests.

In an ideal situation, individuals employ each of these four modes to learn new material. However, in many college classrooms in the United States, professors emphasize reflective and abstract learning methods more often than concrete experience and active experimentation. The same can be true in other educational systems. Study abroad students should keep in mind that their preferred learning style might be different from what their overseas professors routinely expect. For example, many faculty members around the world rely primarily on lecturing as the method of instruction. U.S. American students who prefer discussions in class or hands-on projects might feel frustrated or out of place in a class that meets for two or three hours straight and consists entirely of a lecture. I do not mean to imply that you should rely exclusively on the learning style you prefer or refuse to use the strategies or techniques that are expected in new situations. I do mean to suggest that identifying your own learning styles will help you adapt to your learning environment and find strategies that will help you succeed in your academic and cocurricular work.

Just as each person uses these different styles of learning on a regular basis, you can assume that individuals in the host culture will also prefer various learning methods throughout their life. Some individuals will find "book learning" and reflection the most comfortable ways to learn, whereas others will find those methods frustrating, preferring to participate actively in new situations or experiment with new approaches whenever possible. If you will be studying in a host university while abroad and will be sitting alongside both native and international students, keep in mind that their learning styles and individual strengths will vary, even among those who grew up in the same educational system. Also keep in mind that instructors at the host university may favor one style of teaching (such as lectures and note taking) over other methods of learning (such as class discussion or experimentation) because of their own personal preferences and training.

Learning to adapt to different situations in your classes and being patient with a different approach to teaching and learning will help you develop intercultural skills and awareness.

You as a Cultural Being

Regardless of where you grew up, what schools you attended, or how many people are in your family, you have been shaped by your personal and family experiences and by the world around you. Although we generally do not talk specifically about the cultural values we hold, you have been shaped by numerous values, expectations, beliefs, and norms. All people have a culture, although they might not think of it very much because these expectations and values are deeply embedded in every aspect of their lives.

If you grew up in one part of the country and then traveled to another area for school or employment, you likely noticed differences between how people act, talk, and think from one part of the country to another. An example from my own life illustrates this. When my family and I moved to North Carolina several years ago, we noticed different patterns in how people talk with each other in our neighborhood. In North Carolina, people say "sir" or "ma'am" regularly, sometimes in every sentence. "Hello, sir, how are you today, sir?" comes naturally to many people. In addition, when speaking about teachers or neighbors, it is common to refer to people as Mr. or Miss followed by their first name rather than their last name or family name. I am regularly called "Mr. Steve" in my neighborhood rather than "Mr. Duke." Having spent most of my life in the Midwest and the West, I have needed to adjust the way I speak with people to follow local patterns of speech. I still find it hard to say "sir" or "ma'am" or "y'all" as quickly or as frequently as many people do, but at least I am aware of my own habits and how others speak.

Another example of this is the friendliness of North Carolinians. In our neighborhood, people wave to each other on the street, whether passing each other quickly in cars, walking a dog, or riding a bike. I have noticed that this pattern of waving and being friendly extends to new people and visitors, even those you might not have met. Students, faculty, and staff who move to North Carolina from other parts of the country are often surprised at the openness and friendliness of the people here. Implicit in their shock and surprise is that people in their hometown are more reserved when meeting strangers or walking on the street. Students from New York City or other large urban areas, for example, take a different approach to greeting people than does someone from a rural community.

My point is that you have been shaped by numerous values, expectations, and beliefs in your culture, even if you have not noticed them or articulated them to someone else. As you prepare to study abroad, try to pay attention to your own thoughts and expectations when entering new situations. Do you expect others to shake your hand vigorously or kiss you on the cheek when you meet? Or do you prefer to maintain a proper distance, keep a "straight face," or smile or nod when meeting someone new? The expectations you have and the patterns of thinking or feeling about new situations have been shaped by the culture in which you were raised.

For the culture sleuth, the task is to begin observing the patterns, behaviors, and expectations of people in your host culture. As you notice differences and similarities, it is useful to speak with someone in or from your host culture to discuss your observations and the behaviors of the locals. Talking with others will help you understand the reasons for certain behaviors and the cultural values that shape those behaviors, and it will help the other person to understand your way of thinking.

If you do not have the chance to speak with someone, I encourage you to write down your observations, both about what you witnessed and about your reaction. This "reflection piece" is the part that many leave out of their cross-cultural learning. But self-reflection when encountering new situations is a great way to understand your host culture and to understand your own values, expectations, and beliefs. It will also help you deal with the shocks and surprises that come when living in a different culture.

8

CULTURE SHOCK AND CROSS-CULTURAL ADJUSTMENT

Profile 8: Nicholas Martino

Prior to heading overseas, I had a diverse mix of feelings; I was scared, excited, anxious, and nervous all at the same time. A day did not go by where I did not think about my upcoming trip and what the experience would entail. I had high expectations going into my trip and some pre-conceived notions of Australia as well. While all my expectations were far exceeded, I never imagined the extent I would change, not only as a person but also as a student.

Upon arriving in Australia, I was thrilled to finally be there. I had waited, and dreamed, for so long to come to Australia that to finally be there was incredible. I cannot describe the initial feeling I had touching down in Sydney; it was jubilation, excitement, and wonder all rolled into one. While Sydney was exciting, I was also anxious to get to Perth at the same time; I longed to see the city I had read so much about.

Perth was everything I imagined it to be; the weather was exactly what I expected and more, the people were all very nice and friendly, and the city was as laid back as I had hoped for. I felt more than at home in my first few weeks in Perth; it felt like I had always been in Australia. I felt, literally and figuratively, a world away from the United States and life as I had known it. I told myself, "I can get used to this; I can definitely pick up my things and move here after school is over."

My euphoric state came down to earth when I received my first grade in my linguistics class in Australia. Initially I was petrified at the figure; my sheet read 67 on our first assignment. I started to second-guess my decision to study overseas; I wondered, "If this is supposed to be my easiest class, what will finance or management accounting be like?" I later came to understand the differences in Australian grading (a 67 was considered a B+), but I was still somewhat skeptical of my choice to study abroad. I was still viewing grades through the American prism: A 75 is the bare minimum to pass—any less is failure.

I failed initially to adhere to the Australian grading style, where minimizing loss of points as you accumulate points toward your final mark was the main strategy, whereas, in the United States, students start with the maximum amount of points and are deducted from there. The Australian system favors learning at your own pace; the U.S. system favors structured learning. I had failed, initially, to embrace this change. I soon found out how much better the Australian system played to my strengths as a student.

I came not only to embrace this new school system after my initial resistance but also to flourish in it. I finished with an A, a pair of A-, and a B, all while working at my own pace. I had always been in a structured, focused academic environment, where deadlines were strictly enforced. While the deadlines for work in Australia were also strictly enforced, I had much more leeway and freedom in regard to completing my work. I was given all the assignments at the beginning of the semester and could complete them on my own time and at my own pace. I noticed my stress levels significantly decreased in this system; no longer did I constantly look ahead and cringe at the looming deadlines. I have incorporated this mindset into my studies here at Wake Forest. I have noticed increased retention in my studying without a drop in my class performance, and I have also managed to keep my stress levels down significantly. All in all, the Australian mantra of "no worries" has benefited me greatly, and I have gladly embraced the changes it has brought to me personally and academically.

On a personal level, it was very difficult for me to accept the "no worries" mind-set. For one, it is ingrained into everything we do here in the United States that time is valuable—time is money. If you have free time, or are doing nothing with your time, you are wasting it; you could be doing something productive, anything besides just wasting it. Given this cultural norm, it was very difficult to let go and not stress out over work or continually work even if I was done with all my schoolwork. I felt I always had to do something, anything to ensure I was maximizing my time.

As my experience progressed in Australia, and as I spent more and more time immersed in the culture, I came to understand and appreciate more their mind-set. I felt more comfortable with using my time productively and efficiently rather than using all my time for tasks. We are so focused here in the United States on the bottom line: Time is finite, and we must maximize it. Now, though I do spend a great deal of time on my studies, I have taken more time to simply appreciate the point in life I am in right now: I'm in college, a once-in-a-lifetime event. I won't get back this time or be able to relive this experience. Rather than spend all of my time cooped up in the library or my room doing work, I have taken more time to spend with my friends, go do things I want to do. No longer is my focus solely on "I MUST be doing something at all times." I take time out of my day, or my week, just to relax and enjoy myself; whether it's lying in my hammock somewhere on campus or spending time with my friends, the changes I have experienced have produced a more holistic college experience for me. I am eternally grateful for the opportunity to study abroad. I am extremely pleased that my changes have turned me into a more rounded individual than before.

As I look to life beyond college, I long to take another trip. Currently, I am looking at trips to England or Italy within two or three years after I graduate. Now that I have visited Australia, one of the most iconic and symbolic nations on earth, I cannot wait to see what the rest of the world has in store. I'm sure that no matter where I go in life and no matter the number of places I do visit, Australia will always have a special place in both my heart and my memory. It was my first time outside the United States, and it was the "dream" location, both in my heart and in my mind, to visit. I got more than just a visit though; I left Australia with a changed philosophy academically and socially. I left Australia a changed man.

This volume would be incomplete without a discussion of culture shock and the general process of adjusting to life in a different culture. Each person traveling to and living in another culture needs to adjust to life there in some way. I have told hundreds of students over the past decade that culture shock can be a good thing and that they should look forward to the learning and growth that can come through living in a different country and culture.

Let's first define *culture shock*. Scholars have used this term to describe a sense of shock and disorientation that comes when a person moves into a different culture. The shock comes when a person's expectations, behaviors, or abilities are in conflict with or not in line with what he or she actually experiences in the host culture. This can be caused by linguistic, emotional, psychological, behavioral, or sensory conflicts. In some descriptions culture shock is an overwhelming feeling of overload and internal conflict. However, many study abroad professionals, including me, use the term *culture shock* to describe the general conflict between students' expectations, behaviors, abilities, and emotions and the day-to-day experiences they encounter while abroad. Culture shock can also be described as *transition shock*. By this I mean that the transition between life back home and life in a new country can cause a variety of shocks and surprises. Culture shock can be a positive process when students use a variety of strategies to cope with the stress, to learn about their hosts, and to improve their interactions with the locals.

There are numerous ways in which study abroad students experience a variety of surprises and shocks associated with life in a new country and culture. So many things can be different from what they expect or are accustomed to that many study abroad students have felt overwhelmed, confused, or frustrated. I remember very well the day in Russia when I tried to register my visa with the local authorities but ran into bureaucratic procedures. After waiting in line for nearly three hours, I had just made it to the front of the line when the lady behind the counter slammed the glass window shut and yelled something I did not understand. Later I learned that she had announced her lunch break, which would last for one hour. Everyone else who had been waiting in line simply moved back to the waiting area and sat down. The entire interaction confused me and made me so angry that I stormed off. I later found out that I was in the wrong place and should have gone to an entirely different office to register my visa. This half-day event made me angrier than any day before or after, in large part because I did not understand how the system worked or what I needed to do. I also lacked the words in Russian to understand what was going on, so I was confused.

As you experience shock, surprise, even anger about things that are different abroad, you can also use coping strategies to deal with these stresses and frustrations. This is the process of cross-cultural adjustment. The highly personalized process of learning about yourself and finding strategies that work for the interactions you have in the host culture are key parts of the abroad experience. In contrast to my frustrating experience registering my visa, I can also remember numerous events in Russia when my interactions went smoothly. After doing research in various archives and libraries for several months, I had learned how the systems operated, how to place orders for books and archival materials, what to say to the archival staff, even when and how to eat lunch. I had learned the rules, expectations, and systems, and I had learned the language of the different interactions. Life had improved for me. I am confident that you will also develop new insights, skills, and awareness that will allow you to cope with the challenges and surprises you find abroad.

As you prepare for your program abroad, you will find it useful to learn about the process of cultural adjustment, so you can prepare yourself mentally and emotionally for the kinds of challenges many students face. The following overview of this important topic is intended to give you (and perhaps your family as well) a better framework for anticipating the emotional challenges and stresses that come with living abroad, as well as to recognize the opportunities for personal growth and awareness that come through this process. I will reiterate that culture shock can be a positive process because of the opportunities for learning about your hosts and yourself. Keep in mind that each person's reaction to new experiences abroad is unique and that it is common for students to respond to new situations quite differently, even if they are in the same program or group.

The earliest models of cultural shock and stages of cultural adjustment were developed by Sverre Lysgaard and Kalervo Oberg in the 1950s and 1960s. Since their initial descriptions were published a half century ago, numerous authors have written about culture shock and the process of cultural adjustment and adaptation. The various models and descriptions have generally been lumped into two groupings, which are often called the "U curve" and the "W curve." However, recent research has found these models to be overly simplistic and not reflective of the experience of all individuals who cross cultures (Berardo & La Brack, 2008; Ward, Bochner, & Furnham, 2001). The following description expands on the main ideas of these depictions and includes insights from psychologists regarding the process of culture learning and the development of strategies to cope with the challenges and stresses of life abroad.

Predeparture

Many study abroad students experience a series of emotional ups and downs as they prepare to study abroad. Some have described this as a "roller coaster" experience. You may already have felt a combination of nervousness and excitement as you anticipate going abroad, much like Nicholas, whose profile opened this chapter. The process of picking a program, finding out about others going on the same program, applying for housing, and submitting a visa application can feel daunting and nerve-racking to many students. You are not alone if you feel anxious or nervous about the entire process. This roller coaster experience is common among study abroad students across the world. Many students feel excitement, anticipation, and joy about traveling to a distant country, learning new things, and experiencing the world, much like Heather describes in Profile 3. Other students feel more nervousness or anxiety about the predeparture process.

There are numerous things you can do to prepare yourself to enter a different culture. Several of the strategies that appear in Chapter 2 are particularly useful as you prepare to travel abroad, including learning as much about your host country as you have time for and improving your language abilities. Learning about the food, transportation networks, infrastructure, and other visible aspects of your host culture will give you some background information about what to expect, how to get around, and how to accomplish basic tasks in-country.

Take advantage of every opportunity you have to talk with people from your host country before you go and learn as much as you have time for. Finding an international student, a faculty member, or someone in the community who is from the country where you will study will be beneficial. Doing so will serve to reduce your nervousness and increase your ability to interact with people once you arrive at your program. In addition, it is important to ask questions of your study abroad advisor and program staff and to pay attention to things covered in your predeparture orientation sessions. Remember to read carefully all student handbooks and documents you are given and to pack what you need. Talking with other students who have been on your program can also be helpful as you learn about the program rules and expectations, how to travel to and within your program city, how to access money, and so on.

I also recommend that you learn as much of the local language as you can, regardless of your time constraints. Even if you are going abroad for only one month and have not had the opportunity to study the host language formally, you can still learn how to count from 1 to 10 and how to say basic phrases like "please," "thank you," "excuse me," and perhaps "where is the restroom?" If you have time to learn a few more phrases or to learn the alphabet (even languages that use the Latin script have additional letters not used in English), you will have more tools at your disposal when abroad. You will also be showing respect for your hosts, and many will appreciate that when you interact with them.

Arrival In-Country

Many authors and students have described the initial process of arriving in a foreign country and culture as a honeymoon. Nicholas, whose profile opened this chapter, describes the euphoria and excitement of finally being in Australia. The sights, smells, food, and environment of being in the host culture can be exhilarating, particularly for those who have invested themselves in learning the language or preparing for the experience. This honeymoon phase can last several days or weeks, even if there are a few bumps or shocks along the way. Those who study abroad for a shorter period, say for a two-week visit or short-term summer program, might feel that their entire time abroad feels like a long honeymoon.

How do many students experience this initial arrival phase? For many, the excitement and euphoria of finally being abroad leads them to feel that everything is perfect. The food, the music, and the people seem wonderful. Many newly arrived students write glowing reports to their family and friends about how delicious everything tastes and how beautiful the land and people are. In the arrival phase, it is common for students to focus on the positives of the experience, to highlight the commonalities that they share with their hosts, and to feel that life is wonderful.

However, it is important to note that not every student experiences this euphoria and excitement immediately upon arrival. In fact, I have assisted several students who immediately went into shock or crisis mode upon arrival in-country. One student who studied in Australia for a semester did not get any sleep on the plane during the long flight from the United States, nor was he able to sleep for the first two or three nights. He was overwhelmed by the environment and overcome with nervousness about what he was doing so far away from home. This stress, coupled with exhaustion, put an immediate damper on his experience, and there was no honeymoon for him. Luckily, perceptive staff at the host university recognized what was going on and arranged for a visit with a doctor, the student received some sleeping aids, and within a few days he began adjusting to his new environment. Other students I have known had less successful outcomes, returning home from abroad after just a day or two in-country because they felt completely overwhelmed by the experience of being in a different country or away from family. My main point is that each person is unique, and each person's experience during the first days and weeks of being abroad is unique. If you skip past the honeymoon and go immediately into transition shock, you are not alone.

I should add a caution about drinking too much alcohol during the first few days in the program. Too many students run into significant problems when they are fresh off the plane and feel the thrill and excitement that is common soon after arrival. The newness of being in a different environment plus the lower legal drinking age in many countries have put too many students into dangerous situations because they haven't learned where to go or how people are expected to act in the host culture. In the worst cases, students get drunk on their first night in-country and need to be sent to the hospital or sent home because of poor behavior. Even in moderate cases, way too many students put themselves at risk on the first nights in a program because of excessive drinking and partying and end up losing a phone, camera, money, or some other valuable. Follow the advice of your study abroad program leaders and allow yourself time to adjust to the environment, so you can learn your way around and observe how things work in-country.

Fortunately or unfortunately, the honeymoon generally lasts only a few weeks as students have more interaction with the local population and their transportation systems and institutions and as their expectations and preconceived notions conflict with actions, attitudes, and expectations in the host country.

Culture Shock and Stress

At some point in the first days or weeks of being abroad, many students begin to run into roadblocks or misunderstandings that raise their stress levels. The true "shock" of the experience can start small and build gradually, or it can hit you hard, all at once. Sometimes it is dealing with bureaucracy that provokes this shock, such as registering your visa (this was my case) or paying mandatory government fees. For some students it is the challenge of purchasing food at a market or grocery store, interacting with the neighbors, riding public transit, or doing something similar that brings on the feeling of shock, surprise, or hurt. The short profiles in Chapter 4 were written by students who found the experience of shopping for food unsettling and stressful, because the markets were arranged differently than they had expected. Sometimes what may seem to be trivial things set off an emotional reaction inside of us that is a combination of frustration, anger, and disappointment at how the locals act or how they treat visitors.

The cause for culture shock is generally a disconnect between what people expect will happen in various situations and what they actually experience. For some this might come when a home stay family acts differently or has different expectations than what they had anticipated. For others it might be caused by long rides on a train, subway, or bus, pressed together with people who act or smell different from what they are used to. For others it might be the result of having linguistic problems, having a hard time being understood, or feeling frustrated in understanding why the locals don't respond to situations the way they "should." Weather, temperature (too hot or too cold), and the amount of sunlight (especially too little sunlight in the winter) can also contribute. There are numerous things that can cause stress for study abroad students.

It is common for people going through culture shock or the shock of transition to a new environment to make assumptions about what has happened and why. A common human tendency when people do not understand something that has happened is to form stereotypes regarding the people involved in the interaction. This is particularly the case when they do not understand the reasons why people act the way they do, what values they are expressing, or how their institutions, infrastructure, or social systems work. Some students may think that something is wrong with them or that they have come down with some "cultural disease." However, this is not the case. Culture shock is not a disease but a deep and sometimes frustrating process of adjusting to a different set of cultural norms and values that often includes a breakdown in communication (Weaver, 2000).

In numerous ways, the shocks, surprises, and frustrations that come with the process of adjusting to life in a new country and culture can affect how students act and feel. Some experience symptoms that appear very similar to depression or anxiety. For example, some respond to culture shock or cultural adjustment by sleeping more than usual, sleeping less than usual, drinking too much alcohol, feeling disoriented, crying or complaining, or acting differently than they usually do. If you initially feel out of sorts or homesick in your study abroad country or feel angry, anxious, frustrated, or annoyed at something you have experienced, you are in good company. A vast majority of study abroad students feel something similar at some point in their time abroad. This is a good time to speak with someone in your program about your frustrations and fears, so you can understand their source. Cultural adjustment can be highly frustrating until you understand the sources of your stress and find some strategies to address those issues (the next section contains common coping strategies).

Regardless of the cause of these feelings of shock, frustration, anger, and disappointment, it is important for study abroad students to continue their culture sleuthing, paying attention to how people act, what they say and when, and what their body language and nonverbal actions might signify. Culture sleuths pay attention to the details of what people say or do and look for patterns in that behavior. They also ask questions when there is misunderstanding or conflict and find out what behaviors are expected in those situations. Cana, who wrote Profile 9 (Chapter 9), noticed that she had done something wrong at a restaurant but didn't know why, and she immediately asked one of her hosts to explain what she did wrong. This is an excellent strategy for almost every situation. If you do not feel comfortable asking one of the locals about a situation, speak with your program director or a member of the faculty or program staff. These moments of cultural misunderstanding or conflict actually provide us with significant opportunities for learning about ourselves, as well as our hosts.

Depending on your level of immersion in the culture, your linguistic abilities, and what level of support you have from your program staff and other students, you may experience different forms of culture shock that can last several weeks or even several months. It is common to have days that are a mixture of frustration and happiness, days that are predominantly happy, and other days when you are at your wit's end. Each person is different, and each experiences the shocks and joys of learning a new culture in his or her own time and way. If you are with other students who seem to be doing better than you are with the new language, culture, and expectations, don't despair. The best advice is to endure the frustrations, ask questions, continue being a culture sleuth, and look for meaning amid the similarities and differences you see around you.

Adjusting and Coping

The good news is that the shocking aspects of culture shock do not last forever, although there can be moments of stress and conflict throughout your time abroad. A majority of students who study abroad for a semester or longer gradually begin to adjust to their new environment after a few weeks or months. The adjustment process comes as a result of having patience, paying attention to how people act, learning lessons from speaking with the locals about their expectations and behaviors, finding coping skills that work for most situations, and getting used to how things work in the new environment. Studying and using the local language is a key part of this adjustment process, because doing so improves your ability to get things done and be heard and understood. It can also boost your confidence in interacting with the locals, and this in turn often means that you spend more time with your hosts.

In the U-curve model of cultural adjustment, the adjustment phase begins at the bottom of the U curve as students begin to move out of shock mode and develop some strategies to deal with common frustrations. Another way to describe this is a typical learning curve, where the ability to perform a new task is initially low, then rises gradually before beginning a steady phase of improvement (Ward & Kennedy, 1999). The adjustment process comes as students learn more about the cultural norms and values, become more adept at seeing patterns of behavior around them, and adjust how they act in different situations.

A good model for thinking about these adjustments is called the "ABCs of Acculturation" and focuses on identifying and then using a variety of strategies that will help people adapt to new cultural circumstances. In this ABC model, the *A* stands for *affect* or emotion, *B* stands for *behavior*, and *C* stands for *cognition*. The model works well because it reminds us that multiple levels of change and adjustment are necessary if we want to fully adjust to a new culture (Masgoret & Ward, 2006; Ward et al., 2001).

The ABC model emphasizes the importance of developing coping strategies for the various situations you encounter abroad. Let's start with the *C* for *cognition*. As has been discussed in other chapters, learning more about your study abroad country and hosts will give you more information about their history, political and social institutions, and physical and social environment. Key strategies in the cognition realm include the following:

- Learn about the country and its people
- Learn as much of the predominant local language (or languages) as you have time for
- Read a local newspaper or news website on a regular basis
- Observe what people do when they meet or greet other people
- Pay attention to what you see, hear, and smell in your new environment
- Attend as many cultural events and/or religious services as you have time for, while also being respectful of the local customs

- Interact with the locals as often as possible in order to learn about various aspects of their lives, such as their educational systems, work experiences, social networks, holidays, and traditions
- Ask questions about things you find confusing, interesting, or challenging

Of course, knowing information also implies that you might do something with it. You can adjust your *behaviors* (B) to fit the new environment and common social situations you encounter. Common coping strategies in the area of behavior include the following:

- Adapt how you access the transportation networks to follow the local laws and norms
- Adjust how you interact with men, women, and children in keeping with the patterns that you have observed
- Adjust how you meet and greet people
- Learn to eat food following the local pattern (such as eating with chopsticks, using a fork in your left hand, or scooping food using your fingers)
- Recognize the local patterns for personal space and touching, and try not to freak out when people invade your personal space
- Adjust how you interact with store clerks to fit the local patterns
- Consider adopting clothing patterns that you feel comfortable with (such as wearing a scarf)

The third area of coping strategies, *A*, relates to *affect*, which includes internal emotions, as well as interpersonal style, psychological well-being, facial expressions, and body language. It also includes how you read the emotions and body language of others. Common affective coping strategies include the following:

- Observe what is happening around you when you have a strong negative emotional reaction to a person or event, and then try to identify why you reacted the way you did

- Recognize that things are often unclear or ambiguous when you learn about another culture
- Be patient with yourself as you develop your language skills and learn about the local habits, customs, and expectations
- Take time to chill out when you experience "language fatigue" or feel overwhelmed
- Be resilient and patient with others, even when you become angry
- Write a journal regarding your experiences, focusing on the positive and negative aspects of different interactions
- Speak with other students, faculty, or program staff regarding the challenges and shocks you experience in order to understand cultural differences and stress points
- Consider a different frame of reference when something seems different from what you expected
- Give people the benefit of the doubt when something confuses or frustrates you
- Continue interacting with your hosts, despite any previous negative experiences

As students develop coping strategies for the situations they encounter and as they adjust their thinking and emotional reactions to the local environment, they become more adept in their new surroundings. Adjustment is accompanied by feelings of satisfaction and success at being able to handle things better than they could previously. For many students it brings a sense of independence and emotional confidence that may have been absent just a few weeks before. They may not understand fully how to act or what to say in new situations, but they have more of the linguistic and cultural skills to navigate a wider variety of circumstances. Although they might not recognize the sources of conflict or disconnect, they develop some insights and skills in managing conflicts and being more patient with themselves and others when things seem frustrating or uncertain.

This book is full of profiles written by students who lived through culture shock and challenges abroad. They succeeded in adjusting to the local environment and recovering from the stress and shock of being in a different culture. For example, Teddy (see Profile 10) developed self-reliance by opening himself up to new people and new activities, reading the newspaper, and asking for help. Laura (see Profile 12) found she needed to move outside her comfort zone to meet new people, identify her strengths and weaknesses, and work with her friends to handle new challenges and opportunities. Julianne (see Profile 14) became more independent and confident in navigating London. She took the initiative to join two student clubs and became more spontaneous with her time and friendships.

Adjusting to the major stresses you feel does not mean you won't have any more shocks or stresses. In fact, it is common for students to adjust to certain situations but still have frustrations and stresses in other situations. Adjustment is therefore a gradual process that lasts for several months.

Reentry

Returning home after a semester, a summer term, or a year can be challenging yet rewarding. Many students feel the ups and downs of a roller coaster all over again, just as they did before going abroad. The confidence of adjusting to life abroad and developing new abilities to interact with the locals in a greater number of situations contributes to positive feelings about yourself and your experiences abroad. At the same time, it is common to feel like you have not done all you had planned to do. Wanting to buy souvenirs, visit more places, and take more pictures can leave you anxious about whether you will have enough time to get everything done before getting on the plane. You may also be nervous about how your family and friends will react to you and your stories. You may even miss being abroad even before getting on the airplane!

It is also common for returning study abroad students to experience the same phases of adjustment upon return that they had going abroad. Many students report having a honeymoon phase for a few days while they visit with friends and family, followed by the shock of no longer being abroad and doing the fun things that had helped them learn so much about themselves and the world. Many students have reported feeling unsettled even months after returning home because they miss the people, food, or environment abroad. They developed intercultural skills and newfound strengths and insights about the world, and they are afraid to let those memories or skills go. However, the reentry shock also steadily dissipates as their perspective shifts and they gradually develop new routines.

This is a great time to make plans for additional learning and development. For some this means continuing to study the language they spoke while abroad. For others it means taking additional courses on the history, politics, literature, or arts of their study abroad country. Some students add an international studies minor, whereas others join a Model United Nations club or get involved in a student organization focused on international or global issues. Many students spend more time volunteering, help out at a soup kitchen or homeless shelter, or work with community action organizations to serve in their local communities.

The reentry phase is also a great time to reach out to international students on your home campus. Recent studies have shown that international students have a hard time forming friendships with U.S. American students. Instead, they often spend most of their time with conationals or other international students. You can continue your culture-learning process by eating a meal with international students or inviting them to join a study group. In turn, this will help those individuals learn more about your culture and experiences. They may have questions about why U.S. American students act the way they do, and you can become a "cultural bridge" that helps them find answers to those questions. You will also have additional opportunities to learn about other people and cultures.

One other thing that is unfortunately too common during the reentry phase is the feeling of being isolated or cut off from experiences abroad. Many family members and even fellow students might listen to your stories for 5 or 10 minutes, but then their interest wanes or they change the subject, leaving you feeling unfulfilled or uncertain about your experiences abroad. One student who had studied in Cameroon related that her fellow students wanted to hear the one "most radical" or "most amazing" or "most scary" experience of her semester abroad. She found it hard to put four months of her life into one story. What she really wanted to do was talk in depth about her time abroad and process the knowledge and insights she gained. A common strategy for dealing with this is to seek out other returned study abroad students who may be going through a similar process of reflecting on their experiences and continuing to learn from them, even months later.

Another strategy for dealing with reentry shock is to put together a photo album, journal, or video journal containing highlights from your time abroad. Identify the key events that had the most meaning for you, as well as the individuals who helped you along your way. Write down some of your memories in a story format, highlighting the skills you developed and insights you gained while abroad. Or write a profile similar to those included in this book, describing the "new you" that developed while abroad. Those stories and perceptions of how you grew abroad will be useful down the road when you apply for jobs or graduate school. Documenting your experiences abroad will also help you put those memories into perspective for your own life and development. You will likely find yourself returning to those pictures, videos, and stories for years.

Returning home is also a good time to celebrate all that you accomplished by going abroad. In addition to the courses you took and the language you learned along the way, it is useful to remember the intercultural skills you developed that will benefit you for years to come. The insights you gained about yourself and the world around you will always be useful.

9

ADDITIONAL STUDENT
PROFILES

In writing this book, I reviewed the reflections and stories of many students. Their reflections have been insightful regarding the numerous ways in which they have experienced cross-cultural engagement and developed different intercultural skills. Their stories illustrate not only the variety of study abroad programs and experiences that exist but also the core challenges of cross-cultural engagement. Those students who devoted the time and energy to meet and interact with local people, students at their host university, and even other international students are better able to articulate the intercultural and global awareness that led them to study abroad than students who remain in "the bubble."

Because many students develop new insights about themselves by learning from the stories of others, I have included six additional student profiles in this chapter. These profiles exemplify many of the intercultural skills and awareness that are the hallmark of a globally engaged study abroad experience. For example, Profile 9 reminds us of the importance of observing the actions and reactions of others and of asking questions when things are unclear. Profile 10 illustrates the importance of self-reliance and of learning new information that can expand the types of conversations with local people. Profiles 11, 12, and 14 elucidate the various ways study abroad students develop independence and recognize their own identity and cultural values more clearly. And Profile 13 prompts us to remember that living in a different culture can be fun and eye-opening, particularly when the focus is on observing and understanding the locals, not judging them or criticizing them when they are different from what we expected.

I hope you will enjoy reading these additional profiles. Look for what these students did to learn from their experiences and to reflect on the challenges and surprises they encountered along the way.

Profile 9: Cana Noel

One night in Ghana I went to a fancy restaurant with a group of my friends from Wake Forest and some of the Ghanaian students. We sat around a large table, and there were so many different local dishes in front of us. After we began to eat, the waiter came to take the menus, so I gathered them all together and passed them to him using my left hand. I noticed that the waiter hesitated to take the menus from me, and the other Ghanaians students stared at me and then continued to eat. I didn't understand what I had done wrong. I thought to myself, maybe I wasn't supposed to hand the waiter the menus; maybe he collects them himself. The dinner continued, and we began talking about school, the local food, and music. One of the Ghanaian students asked me to pass him a bowl of rice. Again, I picked the bowl up with my left hand and proceeded to pass it to him. He also hesitated to take it, and the other students gave me this peculiar stare. What was I doing wrong? The other Wake Forest students didn't notice anything, but I felt uncomfortable and confused. I stopped eating and began to just look around the restaurant. The student whom I passed the bowl to asked me what was wrong. I explained to him that I felt as if I did something disrespectful, and I was hoping I didn't offend anyone. He explained to me that the use of the left hand in Ghanaian culture is considered cultural taboo. He explained that this is how it has always been, and people do not use their left hand in any action unless they have no other choice, in which they would say, "Excuse my left hand." I sat there puzzled and feeling terrible. Why did I not know about this huge cultural difference? As far as I know, I had been using my left hand that entire trip, clearly offending everyone I encountered. I wanted to leave the table. I felt so bad that I had committed a cultural sin without even knowing it.

Looking back on the situation, I can see that unawareness, ignorance, and a hesitation to ask questions led to this cultural misunderstanding. Every time I saw an action or any type of behavior that was different in Ghana, I usually just acknowledged that it was different and went on with my day. I wish I had asked more questions to understand why things were done in a certain way to have a better understanding and appreciation for the culture. When I first passed the menus to the waiter and received that reaction, I should have immediately asked one of the students what I did wrong, but I didn't. Failing to ask questions to become aware of something leads to ignorance and at times insensitivity to someone's cultural norms. My first emotional reaction was confusion. I thought, "Why are they acting this way toward me? I didn't do anything." Then I felt terrible when I realized it was something I was ignorant of and that I offended them by doing the action but also by not asking questions to correct my mistake. Being unaware of such an important cultural difference was my problem, not theirs. In my culture we do not have any restrictions in which hand can be used. This is different from the local people; children at young ages are taught this cultural norm and are raised to do everything with their right hand. There was definitely a difference in cultural norms; however, being in a foreign country, I now see that it was my responsibility to recognize and understand these norms. I was a visitor in their country, experiencing their norms and values, and I needed to comply with them, whether I felt the same way or not.

From this experience I learned that in every culture there are cultural norms and traditions that can be subtle, but some can be major distinctions. It is important to be aware of these things before immersing yourself into a new culture. I do know that this incident was a learning experience, and I learned to be more alert and conscious of what happens around me. If I was in the United States and this happened, I probably would not have even noticed the facial expressions of the waiter and the Ghanaian students; however, in Ghana I was more aware of the environment around me. I feel that now that I am home, I should employ this new skill to be able to read people, understand the situations I am put into, and always ask questions when I am unsure. In the future I want to be more aware of cultural differences, and when I notice them I will immediately ask people to show that I am interested in their culture and that I want to learn to be more informed and appreciative of other cultures.

Profile 10: Teddy

Studying abroad was one of the best experiences of my life. That may be a cliché, but it is so true. You learn so much from studying abroad regardless of the country of study. Self-reliance was one of my biggest takeaways from my abroad experience. I cooked most of my meals for myself, planned complicated trips around Europe on my own, and managed to find my way around many European cities on my own. Although going to college helps build some self-reliance, you still end up in a bubble from the real world, where you are with similar people from mostly similar backgrounds. While abroad, I lived with students from many different backgrounds, albeit American. I was able to adapt to the many different friend groups in this living arrangement. This was a pretty substantial change for me, as I usually have a small, very tight-knit friend group and am pretty conservative as to whom I let in. In London, I did not have the security of a tight-knit friend group, so I had to change my approach. I hung out with many different groups of people and managed to have an unbelievable time.

Self-reliance was especially needed when I was visiting other countries. I had to navigate my way around cities, order food, and make friends often while not speaking the native tongue. I found I had to take the initiative and take more chances than usual. Although I am usually the friend to take the initiative, I still tend to be pretty conservative with the initiative that I take. I don't usually take chances. I calculate my decisions. Alone in a foreign country, you have to take chances. I made a fool of myself mispronouncing words in Italian, but if I hadn't done it, I never would have met my friends Leslie and Ana-Flavia in Rome.

Asking for help is also something I have always struggled with, but I think I grew up in this respect while abroad too. I had to ask for help in other countries and at my internship where I didn't know anything about British television before I came to London.

I also became much better at relating to other cultures. I studied the English Premier League so I could talk to the coworkers at my internship more. Additionally I watched a few recommended TV shows such as *Sherlock* in order to connect with them as well.

I gained a global view of world issues. This is definitely something I have resisted since coming home but will have to accept. Often Americans live in this bubble and try not to pay attention to issues outside of it. However, there is an economic crisis currently in Europe. Greece, Italy, Portugal, Spain, and Ireland are all in dire straits. Yet Americans hardly ever talk or think about these countries except in how it may affect us. We don't always realize how great an effect the rest of the world has on us. Talking to Brits, I learned that is definitely something they wanted me to take away from my experience.

One change that I have embraced is reading the newspaper much more often. In London, I read the paper every day on the way to and from work. Now I find myself picking up the *Wall Street Journal* or going to its website daily to stay current on U.S. and world news. It is important to stay informed, as it can help you in class, at your job, and in a social setting. Although I think this is not simply a British trend but also an American one, it is an important change that I have maintained.

Coming home, I definitely value the global perspective more than before. I see the president more as an ambassador abroad. A president's international appeal is a much bigger factor for me now in my voting decision. I hope to factor an international perspective into my job and personal life as well so as to not get boxed into one way of thinking. Global thinking spurs creativity and could allow me to excel over someone without any international experience.

I hope to continue my intercultural competence by keeping in touch with my friends from my internship. I do not know if I will ever get the opportunity to live abroad again, but by maintaining these relationships, I will still have a connection abroad. I will be able to get a different perspective on global issues and even different advice for my life. If I do get the chance to live abroad, I will certainly take it because I know how great a way it is to grow personally. Additionally, I will try to form closer connections with international students to continue to increase my intercultural competence. Although I have learned a lot from my experience, I still studied only in London, which I feel is pretty close to America when compared to other countries. By connecting with other international students, I can gain a broader cultural perspective.

Profile 11: Cameron Rudd

After spending my five months abroad, I realized that a substantial part of me had changed, in the best possible way. I truly was unaware of many of the cultural differences that set us apart and that can be celebrated and experienced while abroad. While Australia has a culture seemingly similar to American culture because of the same language and a generally "Americanized" country, it was in fact very different. This was exciting to me because I was able to experience something radically different in a setting that allowed me to melt into the culture, as opposed to merely looking at it from the outside. I have been to numerous other countries before studying abroad, but I had no idea what I was missing until I saw it firsthand. I traveled to Costa Rica a few years ago, and while this was an incredible experience, I look back now and wonder what the culture was truly like. I spent so much of my time just lying on a beach and enjoying the hotel, but I see now that the culture of a country can be ever-more exciting when you experience it in a way that tourists never can.

Australia is an amazing place that truly changed the way I look at myself, as well as other cultures around me. While I considered myself fairly well traveled before this study abroad experience, I realize now that I have not embedded myself enough in the culture to see the real culture in these countries. In fact, it almost makes me want to go back to these places so I can experience them correctly this time. I can now see a culture for much more than its towns and exports but also for the people and the differences and similarities that we share. Something that I resisted at first was the thought of losing me in the culture. At first, I was afraid to "lose" myself in the Australian culture, but as time went on, I let down my guard and allowed myself to completely embrace this new lifestyle and people as my home. It was a great feeling to have and something that I definitely look forward to bringing with me wherever I go. I resisted this change because I was afraid of losing my identity, but what I didn't realize is that I was actually just adding to my identity and who I am as a person, and this study abroad experience added so much more to me as a person.

If I were to talk about a five-year plan for increasing my intercultural competence, it would definitely include more travel, hopefully to South America. I am very interested in this continent, and I have never been there, so I am hoping to make it there for some time in the next 5 to 10 years. I am fairly well versed in Spanish, so I have a good idea of the culture, although I hope to learn more if I ever go to these places. I want to be able to say that I truly experienced Argentina in a way that cannot be felt in a book or even at a hotel. I definitely am interested in staying with a host family as well.

I consider myself lucky not only after my study abroad experience but also after completing this course about the cultural aspects of an abroad experience. I've learned so much more than I thought I did while abroad, and the conversational aspect of the class truly engaged everyone in ways that I feel we otherwise wouldn't have been able to on our own. I feel that the next time I travel, I will be looking for much different things than I have in the past. I now want to seek out the small cultural parts of a country, not the big touristy things that everyone does. I want to be able to say that I was enveloped by a culture, as opposed to saying that I was merely a guest there for a short period of time. I appreciate everyone's stories this semester because it gives us all a chance to share in things that we experienced. As we discussed in the first few weeks of class, not everyone is very receptive to hearing about our experiences, so it was definitely nice to have this outlet.

Profile 12: Laura Colavita

I was probably around 12 when I heard about studying abroad, and I knew it was for me and that I wanted to do it. The idea just seemed so novel, and it sounded like a one-of-a-kind experience. When it finally came time to go abroad, I was much more nervous than I had anticipated. I hardly knew anyone going, and I had never been to Prague before, plus I wasn't even sure whom I would be living with. I was terrified. But this is what I enjoyed the most. I was so nervous about this new experience because everything about it was going to be so new, and I was going to have to adapt to a whole new world. I adapted very well. I loved it the second we landed. I have always had a fair amount of confidence, but this experience really gave me an extra amount of "umph."

Once I was in Prague I was making tons of new friends, experiencing wonderful aspects of the city, and feeling so confident about it all. I really proved to myself that I can go somewhere on my own and form these great relationships with American and international people and share wonderful memories with them. I really felt in control and was so proud of myself for making it in this new world.

When traveling to other places, many of my friends would be very laid back and relaxed, but I realized that I am not a good traveler. I really resisted that acceptance of not being able to control certain aspects of travel, and I couldn't trust an airline not to lose my bag. Luckily, my friends realized this about me before I even did, so they were patient with me as I packed 10 times over and when I would get anxious in security, and I really appreciate that because I know it must have been frustrating at times.

I have embraced a more accepting outlook on life. I have always been pretty accepting of others, but at the same time I haven't been exposed to too much diversity, so it was never that difficult. I think that it is easier to shut people out and ignore those who are different because then you don't have to face things that can be outside of your comfort zone. I am now more comfortable outside of my comfort zone, and I have had my eyes opened to just how much I can learn from others. I met countless people with the most intriguing backgrounds, and I loved every story that I heard, and I want to hear more. Unfortunately, it is hard to do that here at Wake Forest, but I look forward to finding that diversity and learning more about others through other aspects of my life.

My goals and values have definitely been refined because of my study abroad experience. I have a better understanding of what I want from life. I can better separate petty aspects of my life from more enriching aspects, and I have learned to put more value on the important things. I learned not to care as much about what others think but rather to let relationships form naturally. My best friends from abroad are ones who I felt 100% comfortable around and knew that I could share an infinite number of happy memories with. The ones that I did not feel as comfortable with strengthened my belief in always showing respect to others but not minding them too much because it is important to focus on you and what makes you stronger. I believe I have always thought along these lines, but being in a new situation with a whole new set of people really reiterated many ideas I have about people and friendships.

After being abroad I absolutely want to continue traveling as much and as far as I can. I want to learn as much as I can about people's backgrounds and their cultures. I love it when I am talking with someone and I say to myself, "I've never thought of it that way." It shows how much more there is to learn about life and about others, and it always gives me something fascinating to think about. In the next five years, I do not have anything concretely planned for abroad travel, but I do plan on learning more about different cultures within the United States. I have lived in North Carolina my whole life, so I am very interested to see how other perspectives vary across the states. While nothing is planned for a trip overseas, I'm sure I will make something happen sooner rather than later.

Profile 13: Danny

Last summer I studied in Tours, France, for six weeks. Although the program was only about a month long, it had a very profound outcome on my perspective of life. What differed between my study abroad experience and any other long vacation was that I was sharing the same language for six weeks and living with a French family. Living with a French family was integral in my cultural immersion.

My French family was much different from any other American family I have ever known. The makeup of the household was in itself interesting enough. My host mother was bisexual, and this was the first time I have ever met somebody from an alternative lifestyle. Being somewhat naïve and unfamiliar, unfortunately I have been somewhat judgmental, but I was able to truly appreciate and look beyond the superficial and appreciate people for who they are instead of what they like. This was a big achievement in terms of maturity and acceptance, and I'm glad that I have been able to overlook this.

Studying abroad and being part of a culture other than my own was a very grounding experience, and it forced me to rely on my own strengths at times when I felt lost and out of place. It was great to have a lot of reflective time for myself, and I truly did learn a lot. Unfortunately, this was my only opportunity to study abroad, and I am very glad that I did take advantage of it.

With graduation just a few months away, I realize that my time is running out to study abroad, but I have actually discovered a great opportunity to perhaps further my intercultural experience. I was thinking about actually enrolling in a yearlong program at the same university that I was studying at this summer. It has a specialized yearlong program to immerse the students for French-language training. People from American companies and universities often are sent to the Touraine Institute to become fluent in French. I think that this would be a fantastic opportunity to be immersed for a long duration, and being that I would be going alone rather than in a group, I feel like I will have no other choice but to learn the language and culture and have it be my own for a year. The benefits of doing such a program would be limitless. It would be a great way for me to stand out as a job applicant and prospective banker.

Studying abroad in France for six weeks was one of the best decisions I have ever made. I gained a great understanding for people and a better grasp of the French language and become independent. I would love to find another opportunity to expand my global outlook.

Profile 14: Julianne Hummelberg

Abroad, I become more independent and confident. I was forced into new situations and had to rely on myself. Moving to London and not knowing anyone in the beginning made me confident that I can navigate new situations and challenges calmly.

Applying to the London School of Economics (LSE) also made me confident in my academic abilities. The application process was challenging, and I was given a conditional acceptance. I was forced to raise my GPA in one semester, and this taught me time management and determination. I am now more open to taking on new challenges.

Also, living in the LSE dorm was my first time living alone, so I became more independent and learned to be proactive in meeting new people. Instead of automatically having a roommate and meeting a friend, I had to take initiative meeting people in the building when I first got there. The friends I met in London are now some of my closest friends for life and are from all over the country and the globe. I loved the diverse friend group that I had in London.

I was academically challenged and strengthened my analytical skills. I also gained a truly global economic perspective compared to the more "domestic-focused" economics classes I have taken at Wake Forest. I am using my new global perspective to write my economics honors thesis. I have chosen to write about international trade and how foreign direct investment and trade balances and imbalances can either foster or inhibit growth. Also, adapting to the LSE academic calendar and learning how to deal with large lecturer classes for the first time was interesting. I enjoyed being exposed to different teaching techniques.

While I was abroad in London, I learned more about myself and became increasingly aware of my strengths and weaknesses. Academically and socially, I acknowledged my strengths and interests and really figured out which career path I wanted after college. I joined both business and finance clubs and recognized my strong interest for global financial markets. I then took the initiative to find an internship and am now actively pursuing a career in international finance. Before London I had no idea what I wanted to do after college, but now I am confident in the career path that I have chosen for myself.

I also became more spontaneous abroad. Deciding to take the train to France on Friday two days before, planning last-minute trips to exotic

European destinations, realizing a friend was coming into town that day and planning a perfect day in London: the list goes on and on. I loved the flexible schedule that I had over there and was so excited to experience new places. If class was canceled and I had two extra free hours during that day, I would hop on the tube and discover an area of London I had never seen before. I absolutely loved the excitement of a new discovery each and every day.

Overall, going abroad was the best experience of my life. I became a more motivated, confident person. I now realize my passion for traveling and love of big cities. I am confident in my future career and am excited about the future. Because I had such a positive experience that promoted both intellectual and personal growth, I can't help but advocate how important an international experience is for undergraduate students. I am a peer advisor in the Center for International Studies this year and love promoting my study abroad experience to other prospective students.

IO

CONCLUSIONS

Studying and traveling abroad offers you numerous opportunities for learning and growth. Kudos to you for taking the time and making the effort to see other parts of the world firsthand. In the process of studying abroad or participating in an international internship, service trip, or research experience, you will learn many new things about other countries, ethnic groups, languages, and cultures. You will expand your understanding of the diversity of the human experience and some of the political, social, economic, and historical developments that make each country and group unique. In the process, you will also learn much more about yourself and your expectations and cultural values. You will develop new skills and insights that can be useful for you in the future.

Being aware of the challenges and opportunities for cross-cultural engagement and intercultural skill building is important as you prepare for your program and after you arrive in-country. Cross-cultural engagement is greatly enhanced when you prepare for the experience and when you take the initiative to observe and interact with others. Set goals for yourself regarding what you want to see and accomplish. One of the best strategies for meeting people and developing friendships is to join a club or group within the first two weeks of your arrival in-country. Get outside the bubble as much as you can. As the student profiles demonstrate, when students seek opportunities to meet local people and observe their habits, expectations, and assumptions, they generally feel that they understand the locals much better. As a result, they feel that their program has been more rewarding and that they took maximum advantage of the time they had abroad.

I wish you success in your program and journey abroad.

Things to Know Before You Go

Although this list may seem long, learn as many details as you have time for, both before departure and after arriving at your study abroad location.

Political Systems

- Name of the head of state (president, king, queen, etc.) and prominent members of his or her family
- Names of the head of government (prime minister, president, etc.) and other key government leaders (foreign minister, minister of internal affairs, etc.)
- Format and function of the national government and national legislature
- Names of the major political parties
- Name of the mayor or leader of the city where you are studying
- How frequently national elections are held and when the most recent election took place

Religions and Faith Traditions

- Names of leaders of major religions or faith traditions
- Key beliefs or traditions
- What each religion or faith tradition teaches regarding life, death, and interaction with others

Economy

- Names of major companies that operate in your host country and what they produce
- Major exports or imports

- Common predictions for how well the economy will perform in the next one to two years

Sports and Exercise

- Names of professional sports leagues and the teams located in your host city or region
- Colors and emblems or logos of those sports teams
- Common forms of exercise among the general population

Languages and Ethnic Groups

- Names of major ethnic groups
- Rough proportion of the population that speaks the dominant language
- Languages used to conduct official business
- Languages taught most commonly in schools

Holidays

- Names of major holidays and when they take place
- How people generally celebrate those holidays
- Common foods, music, and art associated with those holidays

Music and Art

- Names of major artists and musicians
- Names of famous artists whose works appear in museums or art galleries

REFERENCES

Association of College Unions International. (2012). Retrieved October 27, 2012, from www.acui.org/content.aspx?menu_id=30&id=10208

Bennett, J. M. (2008). On becoming a global soul: A path to engagement during study abroad. In V. Savicki (Ed.), *Developing intercultural competence and transformation: Theory, research, and application in international education* (pp. 13–31). Sterling, VA: Stylus.

Berardo, K., & La Brack, B. (2008, April). *Theoretically speaking: What will we do once the U- and W-curves of adjustment are retired?* Paper presented at the Forum on Education Abroad annual conference. Retrieved December 28, 2012, from www.forumea.org/documents/WedpmBerardoLaBrack-TheoreticallySpeaking.ppt

British Council, Ipsos Public Affairs, & Booz Allen Hamilton. (2013). *Culture at work: The value of intercultural skills in the workplace.* Retrieved May 21, 2013, from www.britishcouncil.org/sites/default/files/documents/culture-at-work-research.pdf

Deardorff, D. K. (2006). Identification and assessment of intercultural competence as a student outcome of internationalization. *Journal of Studies in Intercultural Education, 10,* 241–266.

Deardorff, D. K. (Ed.). (2009). *The SAGE handbook of intercultural competence.* Los Angeles: SAGE.

Dwyer, M. M. (2004). More is better: The impact of study abroad program duration. *Frontiers: The Interdisciplinary Journal of Study Abroad, 10,* 151–164.

Fantini, A. E. (2009). Assessing intercultural competence: Issues and tools. In D. K. Deardorff (Ed.), *The SAGE handbook of intercultural competence* (pp. 456–476). Los Angeles: SAGE.

Fischer, K. (2013). Your brain on study abroad: The experience changes lives, and neurons, a scholar says. *The Chronicle of Higher Education,* May 31, 2013. Retrieved June 7, 2013, from http://chronicle.com/article/This-Is-Your-Brain-on-Study/139543/

Hall, E. T. (1981). *Beyond culture.* New York: Anchor Books. Original work published 1976.

Hammer, M. R., Bennett, M. J., & Wiseman, R. (2003). Measuring intercultural sensitivity: The intercultural development inventory. *International Journal of Intercultural Relations, 27*(4), 421–443.

Hofstede, G. H. (2001). *Culture's consequences: Comparing values, behaviors, institutions, and organizations across cultures* (2nd ed.). Thousand Oaks, CA: Sage Publications.

Kohls, L. R. (2001). *Survival kit for overseas living: For Americans planning to live and work abroad* (4th ed.). Boston: Nicholas Brealey.

Kolb, A. Y., & Kolb, D. A. (2005). Learning styles and learning spaces: Enhancing experiential learning in higher education. *Academy of Management Learning and Education, 4*(2), 193–212.

Kolb, D. A. (1984). *Experiential learning: Experience as the source of learning and development.* Englewood Cliffs, NJ: Prentice Hall.

Masgoret, A.-M., & Ward, C. (2006). Culture learning approach to acculturation. In D. L. Sam & J. W. Berry (Eds.), *The Cambridge handbook of acculturation psychology* (pp. 58–77). Cambridge: Cambridge University Press.

Norris, E. M., & Gillespie, J. (2009). How study abroad shapes global careers: Evidence from the United States. *Journal of Studies in International Education, 13*(3), 382–397.

Paige, R. M. (2002). Culture definition. In R. M. Paige, A. D. Cohen, B. Kappler, J. C. Chi, & J. P. Lassegard (Eds.), *Maximizing study abroad: A student's guide to strategies for language and culture learning and use* (2nd ed., p. 43). Minneapolis: University of Minnesota, Center for Advanced Research on Language Acquisition.

Paige, R. M., Cohen, A. D., Kappler, B., Chi, J. C., & Lassegard, J. P. (Eds.). (2002). *Maximizing study abroad: A student's guide to strategies for language and culture learning and use* (2nd ed.). Minneapolis: University of Minnesota, Center for Advanced Research on Language Acquisition.

Passarelli, A. M., & Kolb, D. A. (2012). Using experiential learning theory to promote student learning and development in programs of education abroad. In M. Vande Berg, R. M. Paige, & K. H. Lou (Eds.), *Student learning abroad: What our students are learning, what they're not, and what we can do about it* (pp. 137–161). Sterling, VA: Stylus.

Pedersen, P. (1995). *The five stages of culture shock: Critical incidents around the world.* Westport, CT: Greenwood.

Peterson, B. (2004). *Cultural intelligence: A guide to working with people from other cultures.* Yarmouth, ME: Intercultural Press.

Preston, K. (2012). *Recent graduates survey: The impact of studying abroad on recent college graduates' careers: 2006–2011 graduates*. Chicago: IES Abroad. Retrieved May 7, 2013, from www.iesabroad.org/system/files/recentgraduatessurvey.pdf

Spitzberg, B. H., & Changnon, G. (2009). Conceptualizing intercultural competence. In D. K. Deardorff (Ed.), *The SAGE handbook of intercultural competence* (pp. 2–52). Los Angeles: SAGE.

Storti, C. (2009). Intercultural competence in human resources: Passing it on. In D. K. Deardorff (Ed.), *The SAGE handbook of intercultural competence* (pp. 272–286). Los Angeles: SAGE.

Ting-Toomey, S., & Chung, L. C. (2005). *Understanding intercultural communication*. Los Angeles: Rosbury.

Trompenaars, A., & Hampden-Turner, C. (1998). *Riding the waves of culture: Understanding cultural diversity in global business* (2nd ed.). New York: McGraw-Hill.

Vande Berg, M., Paige, R. M., & Lou, K. H. (2012). *Student learning abroad: What our students are learning, what they're not, and what we can do about it*. Sterling, VA: Stylus.

Ward, C., Bochner, S., & Furnham, A. (2001). *The psychology of culture shock* (2nd ed.). Philadelphia: Routledge.

Ward, C., & Kennedy, A. (1999). The measurement of sociocultural adaptation. *International Journal of Intercultural Relations, 23*(4), 659–677.

Weaver, G. R. (2000). Understanding and coping with cross-cultural adjustment stress. In G. R. Weaver (Ed.), *Culture, communication and conflict: Readings in intercultural relations* (Rev. 2nd ed., pp. 177–194). Boston: Pearson.

Zull, J. E. (2012). The brain, learning and study abroad. In M. Vande Berg, R. M. Paige, & K. H. Lou (Eds.), *Student learning abroad: What our students are learning, what they're not, and what we can do about it* (pp. 162–187). Sterling, VA: Stylus.

INDEX

Abigail, 87–88
acculturation. *See* cultural adjustment
adapt, ability to, 1, 15, 26, 31, 56, 57, 58, 74, 80, 86, 87, 93, 95, 118–120, 122
adjustment to new culture. *See* cultural adjustment
The Adventures of Ozzie and Harriet, 33
affect, 111–112
age, 65
Africa, 39
alcohol, 36, 106, 108
ambassador, study abroad students as, 30
ambiguity, 85–86
anger, 102, 108
anticipate differences, 55, 103, 104, 107
anxiety. *See* culture shock
arrival to program, 19, 51, 54, 58, 82, 92, 99, 104, 105–106
art and artistic expression, 37–39, 130
Asia, 40
asking for help or insights
  and direct or indirect communication styles, 75, 77, 78
  importance of, 31, 69, 72, 117, 118–119, 120
  to improve understanding of other cultures, 12, 20, 24–25, 47, 49, 51, 64, 70–72, 80, 83, 85, 86, 90, 104, 108–109, 111, 113, 117, 118–119, 120
  in predeparture, 41, 69, 83, 104
  to reinforce language learning, 21–22, 28,
Association of College Unions International, 12

assumptions, 6, 10, 12, 17–18, 22, 24, 26, 27, 51, 55, 59, 64, 69, 89, 95, 107–108, 127
Australia
  Cameron Rudd's experiences in, 121–122
  grading system in, 99–100
  low-key attitude in, 85
  Nicholas Martino's experiences in, 99–101
  "no worries" mind-set in, 100
  Teddy's experiences in, 121–122
authority, 64–67
awareness, xvii, xvi, xvii, 13, 15, 17, 18, 22, 44, 58, 81, 87, 88, 90, 95, 96, 103, 117, 118, 119–120, 123

banya, 70
Barcelona. *See* Catalonia
bargaining, 56
being a U.S. American abroad, 6
behavior, need to observe, 9, 111–112, 118–119
benefits of studying abroad
  independence, 5
  self-confidence, 5
Bennett, Janet, 12–13
beverages, 36
bicycles, 48
body language, 63, 75, 78, 80, 111–112
bodies, exposure of, 69
bubble in study abroad. *See* study abroad bubble
bridge-building, 30, 61, 114
Buddhism, 43
buses, 49–50

Also available from Stylus

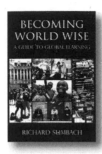

Becoming World Wise
A Guide to Global Learning
Richard Slimbach

"*Becoming World Wise* is a superb resource for educational travelers. . . . Because the content is not country-specific, the book can be used in courses and workshops enrolling students going to any destination. In short, *Becoming World Wise* is an excellent pedagogical tool."—**NAFSA Resource Library**

"This engagingly written book provides helpful guidance to anyone going on an educational, service or mission trip abroad and guidance in how to make the experience an optimum learning experience. Rich in anthropological and sociological insight, this is the perfect book for those who wish to combine travel with learning and service."—**Robert J. Priest**, *Director, PhD Program in Intercultural Studies, Trinity Evangelical Divinity School*

As world travel is growing exponentially, "alternative" travel has grown apace: from ecotourism, gap years, short-term mission trips, cultural travel-study tours, and foreign language study, to college-level study abroad, "voluntourism," and international service-learning.

This book is intended to help the new generation of ethical and educational travelers make the most of their international experience, and show them how to broaden their cultural horizons while also making a contribution to their host community.

Building Cultural Competence
Innovative Activities and Models
Edited by Kate Berardo and Darla K. Deardorff
Foreword by Fons Trompenaars

"*Building Cultural Competence* makes a valuable contribution to intercultural trainers by presenting 50+ innovative activities designed specifically for the development of intercultural competence and framing the use of these activities in terms of intercultural facilitation and intercultural development."—**R. Michael Paige**, *author of* Education for the Intercultural Experience *and Professor of International and Intercultural Education, University of Minnesota*

For HR directors, corporate trainers, college administrators, diversity trainers, and study abroad educators, this book provides a cutting-edge framework and an innovative collection of ready-to-use tools and activities to help build cultural competence—from the basics of understanding core concepts of culture to the complex work of negotiating identity and resolving cultural differences.

22883 Quicksilver Drive
Sterling, VA 20166-2102

Subscribe to our e-mail alerts: www.Styluspub.com